ARCHAEOLOGY

ARCHAEOLOGY
A BRIEF INTRODUCTION

SECOND EDITION

BRIAN M. FAGAN

UNIVERSITY OF CALIFORNIA, SANTA BARBARA

LITTLE, BROWN AND COMPANY
BOSTON   TORONTO

Library of Congress Cataloging in Publication Data

Fagan, Brian M.
    Archaeology : a brief introduction.

    Bibliography: p. 183
    Includes index.
    1. Archaeology.   I. Title.
CC165.F28   1982   930.1   82-12751
ISBN 0-316-25991-8

Library of Congress Catalog No. 82-12751

ISBN 0-316-25991-8

9 8 7 6 5

ALP

Published simultaneously in Canada
by Little, Brown & Company (Canada) Limited

Printed in the United States of America

Produced by Ron Newcomer & Associates

COVER PHOTO: Toltec warrior figure with an *atlatl* and a bag of incense,
one of the roof supports of the Temple of Quetzalcoatl, Pyramid B,
Tula, Hidalgo, Mexico. Photograph by Lesley Newhart.

Credits for illustrations appear on pages 190–191.

To

Lucia, Karen, and other friends at Whittier College who gave me the idea for this book.

And, as usual, to the formidable felines Catticus Rex and Hercules Gryptype-Thynne, who were as subversive as ever. They did everything they could to prevent me from revising the manuscript. As you can see, they failed!

TO THE READER

Archaeology always seems an exciting and romantic subject, especially when you read about the magnificent tomb of the golden pharaoh Tutankhamun or the imposing Maya temples of the Yucatan. Most archaeological sites are less spectacular and are excavated on a far smaller scale. But that does not make them any less fascinating for archaeologist and nonarchaeologist alike. This book is designed to give you some idea of how archaeologists go about studying human behavior of the past. We cover the basic concepts and methods of archaeological research—excavation, survey, analysis of artifacts and food remains, and such topics as dating and the dimensions of time and space. *Archaeology: A Brief Introduction* ends with a look at career prospects in archaeology and at ways individuals—like you—can help save the past for future generations. References for more detailed reading are given at the end of the book.

I hope that this short text will give you new insights into the fascinating world of the past. Good luck with your adventures in archaeology!

TO THE
INSTRUCTOR

This book is designed as a brief introduction to the fundamental principles of method and theory in archaeology. It begins with the goals of archaeology, goes on to consider the basic concepts of culture, time, and space, and discusses the finding and excavation of archaeological sites. The last four chapters summarize some of the ways archaeologists order and study their finds. Throughout the book, I emphasize the ethics behind archaeology. We end with the vital question of how nonarchaeologists should relate to the finite resources that form the archaeological record. In my experience this subject is often neglected in introductory anthropology courses.

Our assumption is that this small book will act as supplementary reading for a general course in anthropology, and that your students will spend two or three weeks on the subject matter. Every attempt has been made to keep technical jargon to a minimum. Inevitably, a book of this length and scope glosses over many complex problems or smoldering controversies. I have proceeded on the assumption that a positive overstatement is better than a complex piece of inconclusive reasoning, at this stage in learning. Errors of overstatement can always be corrected in class or at a more advanced stage.

If there is a theme to *Archaeology*, it is that the patterning of archaeological artifacts we find in the ground can give us valuable insights into human behavior in the past. In pursuing this theme, I have attempted to focus on the basic concepts of archaeology. I leave you to impose your own theoretical viewpoints on the various chapters that follow. My assumption is, too, that you will fill in such additional details you feel your students need. For this reason, I have drawn again and again on a few well-known sites from New and Old World archaeology, such as Olduvai Gorge and Teotihuacán, rather than distracting the reader with a multitude of site names.

Space limitations prevent us from referencing the entire text. A short guide to further reading appears at the end of the book.

The second edition of *Archaeology* has benefited from the comments of dozens of instructors and students. The resulting changes are relatively minor. The sections on human culture, seriation, and sampling have been rewritten, some minor errors have been corrected, and sites and chronologies have been updated. We have changed some illustrations and brought the references up to date. In general, however, the book has stood the test of time well, for the basic principles it covers alter little from year to year. They provide the foundation for all the multifarious research projects that archaeologists carry out, as near home as California and as far away as Mongolia.

I am grateful to all those who criticized the first edition, sent me information, or read portions of the revised manuscript. My grateful thanks to Professors Charles Cecil of San Jose City College, Malcolm Webb of the University of New Orleans, and Claire M. Cassidy of University of Maryland, College Park, who reviewed *Archaeology* before revision. Any suggestions for improving future editions of this book would be greatly appreciated.

CONTENTS

1. **ARCHAEOLOGY AS ANTHROPOLOGY**   1

    Archaeology   **2**
    Types of Archaeology   **8**
    Human Prehistory   **11**
    Anthropological Archaeology   **16**
    The Goals of Archaeology   **19**

2. **CULTURE AND THE ARCHAEOLOGICAL RECORD**   **23**

    Human Culture   **24**
    Cultural Systems   **26**
    Cultural Process   **27**
    The Archaeological Record   **30**
      Archaeological Sites   **32**
      Artifacts   **33**
    Context   **36**

3. **TIME**   **38**

    Relative Chronology   **40**
      Artifacts and Relative Chronology   **41**
      Cross Dating   **45**
      Relative Chronology and the Ice Age   **47**
    Dating in Years (Chronometric Dating)   **51**
      Historical Records and Objects of Known Age   **51**
      Tree-ring Dating (Dendrochronology)   **52**
      Radiocarbon Dating   **54**
      Early Prehistory   **57**
      Potassium Argon Dating   **57**

4.   **SPACE**   59

The Law of Association   **61**
Subassemblages and Assemblages   **63**
Households, Communities, and Activity Areas   **66**
Culture Areas and Settlement Patterns   **67**

5.   **PRESERVATION AND SURVEY**   71

Preservation   **72**
Finding Archaeological Sites   **76**
Deliberate Archaeological Survey   **78**
Aerial Photography   **82**
Remote Sensing   **84**
Accidental Discoveries   **86**

6.   **EXCAVATION**   89

Excavation   **90**
Research Design   **91**
Types of Excavation   **93**
   Vertical Excavation   **96**
   Area Excavation   **97**
Digging, Tools, and People   **98**
Recording   **100**
Habitation Sites   **101**
   Hunter-Gatherer Campsites   **101**
   Caves and Rockshelters   **103**
   Mounds   **104**
   Earthworks and Forts   **105**
   Shell Middens   **106**
Ceremonial and Other Specialist Sites   **106**
Burials and Cemeteries   **107**

7.   **ORDERING THE PAST**   111

Back from the Field   **112**
Classification and Taxonomy   **113**
   Attributes   **114**
   Natural Types   **116**

Analytical Types   **118**
Attribute Clusters   **119**
Units of Ordering   **120**
Larger Archaeological Units   **123**
Explanatory Ordering   **124**
Cultural Process   **125**
Inevitable Variation and Cultural Selection   **125**
Invention   **126**
Diffusion   **127**
Migration   **128**
Cultural Ecology and Cultural Process   **129**

8.   **SUBSISTENCE**   **131**

Evidence for Subsistence   **132**
Prehistoric Diet   **133**
Animal Bones   **134**
Animal Bone Analysis   **135**
Game Animals   **135**
Domesticated Animals   **136**
Aging and Butchery   **137**
Vegetable Remains   **139**
Birds, Fish, and Mollusks   **142**
Rock Art   **145**

9.   **INTERACTION**   **147**

Settlement Patterns   **149**
Structures   **149**
Communities   **151**
Catchment Areas   **153**
Site Interactions and Distributions   **156**
Site Hierarchies   **157**
Central Place Theory   **158**
Trade   **159**
Social Organization   **161**
Artifact Patterning and Settlement Patterns   **162**
Religious Beliefs   **164**

10.   **ARCHAEOLOGY TODAY AND TOMORROW**   **168**

The Living Past   **169**
Comparisons   **170**
Living Archaeology   **171**
Experimental Archaeology   **175**
The Future of the Past   **176**
Archaeology and You   **178**

FURTHER READING   **183**

INDEX   **193**

1

ARCHAEOLOGY AS
ANTHROPOLOGY

Archaeology is the special concern of a certain
type of anthropologist.

JAMES DEETZ, 1967

ARCHAEOLOGY

"Archaeology is the science of Rubbish," wrote British archaeologist Stuart Piggott some years ago. His definition
conjures up a pleasing image of archaeologists delving
deeply into innumerable ancient rubbish heaps. Piggott is
partly right. Many archaeologists do spend their time digging up long-abandoned rubbish, and sometimes even modern garbage. But the popular image of an archaeologist is
somewhat more glamorous — the archaeologist as treasure
hunter. Everyone has seen cartoons of the bearded, bespec-
tacled archaeologist digging in the foundations of a mighty
pyramid.

Then, too, our complex world is full of "unexplained"
mysteries and hidden surprises. Many people believe that
the archaeologist lives in the mysterious regions of our
world, with grinning skeletons, "missing links", and long-
lost civilizations. Enterprising authors and movie producers
take us on fantasy rides into these strange territories of their
specially selected archaeologists. From the comfort of our
armchairs, via television, we can search for lost continents,
reconstruct Noah's Ark, and trace the landing patterns of
extraterrestrial astronauts' spaceships. Such searches for "lost
mysteries" are not only fantasy fun but big business as
well. Millions of dollars have been made from this type of

archaeology, though, unfortunately, this world bears little resemblance to reality.

The romance of archaeology has taken people all over the world in search of the past. Thousands of tourists visit the pyramids of Gizeh in Egypt every year (Figure 1.1). The Mexican government spent millions of pesos on a restoration of the ancient city of Teotihuacán in the Valley of Mexico to promote tourism. Most popular package tours abroad now include visits to an archaeological site or two (Figure 1.2). Many sites, like Stonehenge in England, are in danger of permanent damage from the sheer numbers of tourists that visit them. Any thinking person who visits an archaeological site faces the reality of the past, a vista of human experience that stretches back far into remote time. How, visitors may wonder, do archaeologists know how old a site is, and what do the finds made in their digs mean? It all seems very complicated to dig for the past. And the unchanging, incredibly ancient structures that surround one add to one's sense of romance and awe.

FIGURE 1.1 The pyramids of Gizeh in Egypt. "The romance of archaeology has taken people all over the world in search of the past."

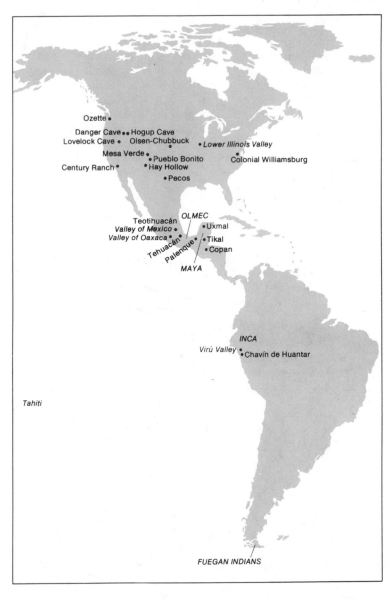

FIGURE 1.2 The archaeological sites mentioned in this text. Obvious geographic place names are omitted.

4

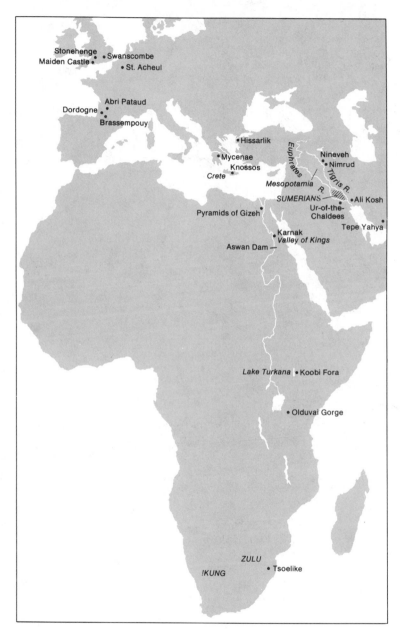

5

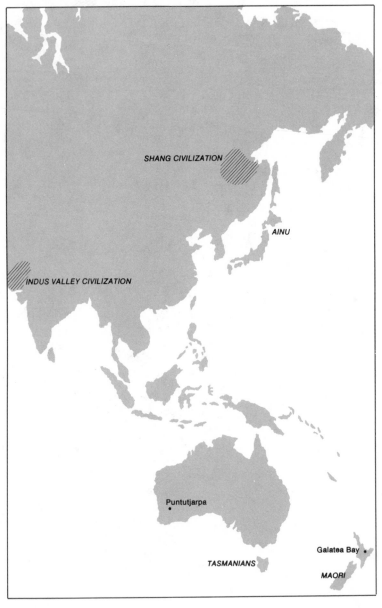

SHANG CIVILIZATION

AINU

INDUS VALLEY CIVILIZATION

Puntutjarpa

Galatea Bay

TASMANIANS

MAORI

Most such archaeological sites now boast a museum. Eagerly, the tourist leans over the display cases and admires the glittering gold of a fine necklace or the crude stone tools made by a human hand over a million years ago. Perhaps, at the door, our tourist pauses to buy a replica of the archaeological find in the case. It serves as a pleasing reminder of a fleeting visit to the past, a memento to be displayed to admiring friends at home. But, unfortunately, many people are greedier. They covet the past and want to own a piece of the real thing for themselves.

Collectors and treasure hunters are the curse of archaeology. Many of them regard themselves as legitimate archaeologists. The vanity of our ancestors decreed that they be buried with their riches to accompany them in the afterlife. The greed of their descendants decrees that people today covet these riches. The antiquities dealer and the private collector pay enormous prices for pre-Columbian pots and other fine antiquities looted from otherwise undisturbed sites. Major museums compete to acquire the finest specimens of prehistoric art. The Metropolitan Museum of Art in New York recently paid a cool million dollars for a Greek vase.

There seems to be some fundamental human desire to collect things and display them in the privacy of one's home. Collecting is a passion once described as "so violent that it is inferior to love or ambition only in the pettiness of its aims." People collect everything, from barbed wire to beer cans, and many think of archaeology as the acquisition of objects. But when people collect archaeological finds, they are collecting a part of a finite resource that is rapidly vanishing, a unique archive that can never be replaced. Every object they buy or dig from a site is the product of ancient human behavior. This behavior can be partly reconstructed from objects found in the soil, but much of our insight depends on the **contexts** (positions) in time and space in which the objects occur in the ground. Removing an artifact from its context is an irreversible act that cheats us all of knowledge.

Modern archaeology is not treasure hunting, nor is it a fantasy search for lost worlds. *It is the systematic study of the material remains of human behavior in the past.* The bearded archaeologist of cartoon fame has been replaced by scholars with broad training in many skills who study prehistoric behavior. **Prehistory** is *that portion of human history that extends back before the time of written documents and archives.* Prehistoric archaeologists are that special breed of archaeologists who study human prehistory.

TYPES OF ARCHAEOLOGY

There are, of course, many types of archaeologists. Many people associate archaeologists with Greek and Roman temples, with Classical statuary and ancient art, with Egyptian pyramids and mummies. Such studies are the work of **Classical archaelogists.** Many are predominantly art historians who happen to use archaeological methods to recover data from the ground. Classical archaeologists work hand in hand with documentary historians. For the most part, they are concerned with the objects they dig up, as fine examples of Classical art. They have relatively little interest in the minute economic and social problems that interest prehistoric archaeologists.

Historical archaeologists study sites that date to recent, historical times. Some excavate cities like Saxon London or medieval Winchester, which flourished in the dim yet documented past. American historic-site archaeology revolves around pioneer settlements, like Colonial Williamsburg, Spanish missions in the Southwest, or nineteenth-century frontier forts. Scholars at these sites are frequently concerned with such objects as pottery imported from England, Italy, and China, and Spanish-style architecture and uniform buttons. Some archaeologists study factories or slum housing dating from the Industrial Revolution or even later.

In all these cases, the archaeologist fills out details lacking in historical records. Contemporary historical records are usually concerned with political and religious matters, with the deeds of civic leaders and statesmen. They rarely describe ways in which people lived, the meals they ate, or where their toilets were located. Hundreds of small cottages huddled within the walls of medieval Winchester in England, for example. Their owners plied their crafts, quarreled with others, even went to court to settle their differences. Court records and title deeds provide the names of the cot-

FIGURE 1.3 Excavations at Colonial Williamsburg. Historical archaeology was used here to discover details of a Colonial mental hospital.

tage owners and the details of their law cases. The archaeologist can learn more about them, tracing the long-forgotten foundations of their houses. Much of historical archaeology results in the reconstruction of ruined buildings as part of our national heritage. Colonial Williamsburg, Virginia, is the most famous of early American towns. It has been reconstructed with active help from archaeologists (Figure 1.3).

Underwater archaeologists study ancient wrecks in the Mediterranean, around Florida, and elsewhere. Special recording techniques have been developed to recover the smallest details of shipwrecks and the cargoes in their holds. Unfortunately, many people believe that wrecks contain rich treasure and golden doubloons. Thus, many wrecks have been robbed or destroyed by inquisitive divers long before archaeologists can get there.

Archaeology has been used to study modern households, too. Using methods developed for studying prehistoric rubbish heaps, archaeologist William Rathje has delved into thousands of Tucson, Arizona garbage bags, studying the waste disposal of lower-, middle-, and upper-income households. He found, for example, that everyone discards rubbish indiscriminately, that low-income families consume the most vitamin pills, and that the average Tucson family wastes about one hundred dollars' worth of beef a year. The implications of this research for consumers and manufacturers are fascinating. The Tucson project has also provided useful theoretical information for the study of ancient middens (garbage heaps), even if Tucson itself happens to be several sizes larger than ancient Nineveh or Teotihuacán.

In contrast to Classical and historical archaeologists, **prehistoric archaeologists** deal with an enormous time scale of human cultural evolution that extends back at least four million years. Prehistoric archaeology is the primary source of information on 99 percent of all human history. Prehistoric archaeologists are concerned with how early human societies all over the world came into being, how they differed from one another, and, in particular, how they changed through time.

The prehistoric archaeologist has to be a specialist in a specific area and time period. No one could possibly become an expert in every aspect of prehistoric archaeology. Some specialists deal with the earliest humans, working closely with geologists and anthropologists who are interested in human biological evolution. Others are experts in stone toolmaking, in the early peopling of the New and Old Worlds, or in the life-styles of hunter-gatherers. Specialists in the origins of agriculture or urban civilization work closely with experts on topics ranging from architecture to cattle. The best archaeological excavations are those which involve the cooperation of a whole team of scientists working together to study prehistoric settlements in the context of their environments. We shall give many examples of this type of research below.

HUMAN PREHISTORY

Until comparatively recently, scientists believed that the Biblical legend of the Creation was absolutely true, and that God had created the earth in seven days. In the seventeenth century, Archbishop James Ussher calculated from the scriptures that the world was created in 4004 B.C. This timetable left only six thousand years for all of human existence. It was not until 1859 that Charles Darwin's theory of natural selection provided an alternative explanation of the origins of humankind, one that allowed a much longer time scale for the presence of humans on earth.

By that time, too, archaeologists had found crude, humanly made stone axes in the same geological beds as the bones of long-extinct animals. Clearly now, people had been living on earth far longer than six thousand years. But how long had they been around? When and how did the first humans evolve? Was there a "missing link" between humans and apes? The great biologist Thomas Huxley posed the question eloquently: "The question of questions for mankind, the problem which underlies all others, and is more deeply interesting than any other — is the ascertainment of the place which man occupies in nature and of his relations to the universe of things."

This was not the only problem. How had early humans settled the world and evolved so many different societies? When the Spaniards reached the New World in the fifteenth century, they came across flourishing human societies that appeared to have been in existence for millennia. The Europeans did not know what to make of these people. (Hernando Cortés and his conquistadors managed to obliterate the remarkable Aztec civilization of Mexico in a few short months.) Some Spaniards questioned whether the Indians were human at all. When it was established that they were, the problem became one of relating them to the Biblical story of the Creation, and the Garden of Eden. Had all humankind descended from one stock? If so, how had the American Indians gotten to the New World?

By the end of the nineteenth century, most scholars agreed that the earliest Americans had probably arrived in the New

World via the Bering Strait. But how long ago had they crossed its arctic waters? When did the first hunter-gatherer bands settle on the Great Plains and in Patagonia? When archaeologists found stone arrowheads next to the bones of extinct animals in New Mexico in 1924, they knew that early Indians had been hunting large, long-vanished mammals. But still, half a century later, no one knows just how long ago the first Americans crossed from Asia.

Many other areas of the world remain as much of a mystery, for the first peopling of the globe is still imperfectly understood. Prehistoric archaeologists are trying to document and understand the ways in which humanity adapted itself to the many and diverse environments of the globe. By studying these adaptations, we can begin to understand the astonishing diversity of human cultures that make up our own world.

As archaeologists began to study the prehistory of humankind, a new breed of social scientist, the anthropologist, was beginning to look at the many strange and diverse societies that explorers and missionaries were revealing every year. They ranged from the simple hunter-gatherer societies of the Tierra del Fuegan Indians and Australian aborigines to the more complex and well-organized societies of the Japanese Ainu and the Pueblo Indians of the American Southwest. Then there were the ancient Egyptians and the Sumerians of Mesopotamia, whose societies could be directly linked to early Western civilization. How could one explain all this great diversity?

In the 1870s, the great British anthropologist Edward Tylor attempted to do so. He organized humankind into three stages of achievement. The earliest prehistoric bands were obviously hunter-gatherers. He grouped them with modern hunter-gatherers in a state of *Savagery*. Much later peoples cultivated crops and tamed animals. They moved around less than their predecessors and lived in more elaborate societies. Tylor described such people as being at a stage of *Barbarism*, a far cry from modern civilization, but more advanced culturally than mere Savagery. Tylor considered his own Victorian society to be the ultimate pinnacle, which, at least theoretically, all human beings sought to reach. So he named his most advanced stage *Civilization*. The Sumerians and ancient

Egyptians were the earliest of civilizations. Human societies, argued Tylor, had progressed through these stages on their way to modern civilization.

But if some peoples had progressed, how had they first become farmers and cattle herders or become civilized? Both these major developments have been studied intensively since the 1870s, for they are rightly regarded as major milestones in prehistory.

The first scholars to speculate about early agriculture assumed that both the first civilizations and the earliest farmers had emerged in the Near East. So they searched for the village occupied by a brilliant genius who had first planted the soil and watched precious wheat grains germinate into a new and predictable food supply. No one has ever found this mythical genius. We now realize that farming and the domestication of animals were changes in human culture that took place over thousands of years, not only in the Near East but in other areas of the world as well. Throughout prehistory, human societies experimented with new ideas and technologies. Only a few caught on, and only a handful — among them agriculture, metalworking, writing, and wheeled transport — have had a radical effect on culture.

Even the Greeks and Romans assumed that the ancient Egyptians were the earliest of all human civilizations. They pointed to the silent pyramids of Gizeh rising above the banks of the Nile, to the great learning of Egyptian priests. But it was in fact the Mesopotamian delta between the Tigris and Euphrates rivers that saw the emergence of the world's first city states and urban communities more than five thousand years ago. Sumerian civilization boasted of fine public buildings, great temples and many priests, and a distinctive written script that soon evolved into wedge-like cuneiform writing. From the Sumerians, a continuous historical record takes us from Mesopotamia through Biblical times right up to the conflicts and astonishing economic and technical achievements of Western civilization. Western colonists and missionaries were soon encountering and overwhelming the mighty civilizations of the Aztec and Inca. They befriended and exploited the Virginia Indians and accelerated the extinction of what they called "primitive people" all over the world.

Most prehistoric peoples did not resist the onslaught of Western civilization long. The Tasmanians lasted precisely seventy years before they were hunted into extinction. The Indians of Tierra del Fuego were decimated by whale hunters and disease; they managed to survive until this century, a scant four hundred years after their first encounters with Europeans. Many prehistoric tribes in Africa, the Amazon Basin, and the Philippines confronted Western civilization for the first time only within the last century. As fast as Westerners encountered alien societies, they sought to mold them to their own concept of what a "civilized" human society should be. Archaeologists in turn assumed that theirs was the only civilization to create the great inventions of humankind.

But as world travel became easier, and the bewildering diversity of humankind became more familiar, archaeologists looked further afield than the narrow horizons of the Near East. The archaeological researchers of this century have revealed a wide array of prehistoric human societies, as fully varied as the picture of living peoples revealed by eighteenth- and nineteenth-century explorations. People are now beginning to think in terms of a true world prehistory, one that amplifies and extends the scope of written history back into the unknown all over the globe.

We now know, for example, that complex prehistoric civilizations flourished by the Indus River in Pakistan, in northern China, and in North America, Mexico, and Peru. The Cretans and Mycenaeans enjoyed a prosperous civilization about 3,500 years ago. African rulers held sway over enormous empires in tropical Africa over the last two thousand years. Few human experiences are unique, and parallel developments in many parts of the world should come as no surprise. No longer can one agree with Edward Tylor and other pioneers that all humankind evolved in well-regimented stages from Savagery through Barbarism to an ultimate state of Civilization.

Only the smallest fraction of all these major developments in human history are adequately recorded in historical archives. The long millennia of human prehistory stretch back into the past from the earlier limits of recorded history in the Near East some five thousand years ago. In many parts of the world, recorded history has an even shorter time scale. The first written records of North American Indian society date from the fifteenth century A.D. The Tahitians of Polynesia first came into written history in A.D. 1767, many African peoples as late as A.D. 1890. Except for some folklore and historical traditions handed down by word of mouth from generation to generation, the only source of information about these, and many other prehistoric peoples, comes from the ground — from long-abandoned settlements and burial sites.

Human prehistory, then, extends from the very earliest settlements of the first toolmaking hunter-gatherers right up to the beginnings of historic urban civilizations and, in many places, into our own times (Figure 1.4). It is that particular type of anthropologist known as a prehistoric archaeologist who studies the major developments of prehistory and places them in accurate contexts of time and space.

ANTHROPOLOGICAL ARCHAEOLOGY

Anthropology is a discipline for the study of humankind in the widest possible sense, both in the past and in the present. Like archaeologists, anthropologists too are often thought of as solitary fieldworkers studying primitive tribes in remote jungles and on Pacific islands. Anthropology has a long and distinguished record of such studies conducted by remarkable people like Franz Boas, who worked among the American Indians, Bronislaw Malinowski, who worked in the Trobriand Islands, and many others. Today, however, there are many types of anthropologists studying all manner of specialized topics. Social anthropologists are primarily concerned with social organization and the more intangible aspects of human society. **Ethnographers,** on the other hand, study technology and economic life, in addition to collecting data on social organization and other aspects of human culture. The **ethnologist** generalizes from the information collected by the ethnographer. The **physical anthropologist** is concerned with human biological evolution and the behavior of humans and their closest relatives. Then there are medical, psychological, urban, and other anthropologists who study various aspects of modern industrial and nonindustrial

cultural anthropology ? ←

FIGURE 1.4   Major events in prehistory referred to in this text.

Modern times	A.D. 1492; Columbus lands in New World
A.D. 1	Teotihuacán, 200 B.C. to A.D. 750 Emergence of Maya civilization, *ca.* 200 B.C.
1200 B.C.	Emergence of Olmec society in Mexico
1600 B.C.	Cretan and Mycenaean civilization in Mediterranean Shang Dynasty in China
2700 B.C.	Emergence of Indus civilization in Pakistan
3000 B.C.	Origins of cities and civilization in Egypt and Mesopotamia
6000 B.C.	Origins of agriculture in the Americas (Tehuacán Valley)
10,000 B.C.	Beginnings of agriculture and animal domestication in the Near East and Southeast Asia
25,000 years ago	Colonization of the New World (? date uncertain)
35,000 years ago	Emergence of modern humans *(Homo sapiens sapiens)*
70,000 to 1 million years ago	Hunter-gatherers people the world
1.5 million years ago	Olduvai Gorge
4 million years ago	Origins of humankind?

society. Archaeologists are anthropologists as well; their goals are the same as those of their colleagues. But their concern is with ancient societies, with cultures that existed in the past and are now extinct or in existence only in a modified form.

The close ties between archaeology and anthropology were demonstrated very dramatically in the southwestern United States a century ago. Swiss-born Adolph Bandelier spent years wandering through the Southwest on a mule. He acquired an encyclopedic knowledge of Pueblo Indians and their recent history, both from Indian informants and early Spanish records. As he put it, he worked back from "the known to the unknown, step by step." Mission records, word-of-mouth histories from tribal historians, modern pottery and ancient potsherds (pot fragments), all were a jigsaw puzzle of information that formed the early history of the southwestern Indians. Bandelier regarded archaeology as a means of extending anthropology into the more distant past.

So did Frank Hamilton Cushing, a pioneer ethnologist who spent five and a half years living among the Zuni Indians in their remote pueblos. He dressed like a Zuni, learned their language, was admitted into their secret societies. Everywhere he looked, he saw a well-organized and long-lived society whose architecture, artifacts, and lifeways stretched back far into the past. Archaeology, he said, was "ethnology carried back into prehistoric times."

So when archaeologists began to dig into the long-abandoned pueblos spotted by Bandelier and Cushing, they traced the pottery styles and architectural designs of the pueblos back from modern times into earlier, prehistoric centuries. To do so, they built on Bandelier's work. They excavated and used the many layers of occupation in ancient and modern villages as a means of developing a time scale for prehistoric cultures. And when the famous archaeologist A. V. Kidder dug extensively into Pecos Pueblo in New Mexico in 1916, he used thousands of pot fragments and other small finds to develop an extremely precise time framework of southwestern prehistory that carried these pioneer efforts to their logical conclusion. The theoretical concepts of anthropology, as well as archaeology itself, have subsequently provided a framework for looking at pre-Columbian

Indian cultures, not only in the Southwest, but all over North America (Figures 1.5 and 1.6).

One big message in this book is that archaeology is much more than the study of objects dug up from the ground. As Bandelier, Kidder, and their successors have shown, archaeologists and anthropologists are concerned with human behavior in all its fascinating variety. Archaeologists look at their finds not merely as objects to be examined and admired, but as vital parts of the extinct society which made

FIGURE 1.5   Pueblo Bonito, New Mexico, a southwestern Pueblo site dated to A.D. 919–1130. The round structures are kivas, subterranean ceremonial rooms.

them. And our ultimate goal, as archaeologists and anthropologists, is to study human society, not objects.

THE GOALS OF ARCHAEOLOGY

Anthropological archaeology is commonly agreed to have three important goals: (1) the study of culture history, (2) the reconstruction of ancient life-styles, and (3) the investigation of ways in which human cultures changed in prehistory.

Our knowledge of **culture history** comes from the study of archaeological sites, and of the many manufactured tools, houses and other structures, and also food remains found there. Groups of sites and their excavated contents must be

FIGURE 1.6   Rain dance at Zuni pueblo. A photograph taken by D. A. Cadzow in the early twentieth century.

described. The archaeologist orders these sites and finds into a time sequence; the distributions of settlements and many different objects are plotted on maps and diagrams (Chapter 7). These descriptive operations yield sequences of prehistoric sites and cultures that may cover a period of a few centuries in a single valley or thousands of years of prehistoric time in an entire region. Once these sequences are set up in space and time, one has a basis for observing changes in human culture over time.

In the traditional view of culture history, archaeologists are anthropologists who describe the *surviving remains* of human behavior in the past. Since preservation conditions in the soil are poor, only the most durable of human tools survive there. Thus, many archaeologists who share the traditional view of culture history believe that it is pointless to look for the more perishable aspects of human culture — social organization, religious beliefs, and so on. This belief has led many archaeologists to limit themselves to classifying hundreds of sites and tools. The result is dozens of sequences of carefully ordered sites described in thousands of scientific papers, and museum storerooms full of rows of humanly manufactured tools. These tools, and other objects, have been described like lifeless catalogue items rather than being regarded as the products of inventive human minds.

During the 1950s, more and more archaeologists began to realize that this was not enough. They argued that prehistoric societies had undergone major changes as a result of ecological and environmental factors. The many different finds which they had classified into sequences of human culture gave, at best, a very limited picture of these prehistoric societies. So they started to look at ways in which people made their living, at ways they exploited their natural environment. Instead of just examining manufactured tools, they studied broken animal bones, tiny seeds, and other food remains that had survived alongside the artifacts. All of these foods had been selected from the natural environment: local environment was a critical backdrop to all human cultures. Environment affected not only food supplies and life-style, but the pattern of human settlement on the landscape as well. The soils, vegetation, water supplies, as well as geography had all played a role in shaping the life-style of the prehistoric inhabitants who exploited it.

One of the first archaeologists to realize this was Gordon R. Willey, who carried out a pioneer study of human settlement in the Virú Valley, Peru, in 1948. Many months of survey with aerial photographs, on foot, and by jeep showed how the inhabitants of the valley had relied more and more heavily on irrigation agriculture and how their settlements had become larger and more sedentary through time. Many archaeologists have followed his example, with settlement studies in Mexico, North America, and many parts of Europe and the Near East.

But the settlement patterns and life-styles of prehistoric societies are, in turn, only part of the picture. Such reconstructions of ancient life-styles were descriptive of human societies' constant interactions with an ever-changing natural environment. But few archaeologists made any attempt to explain *why* the many changes in prehistoric culture and society they observed took place.

Then in the 1960s, archaeology underwent a major change in its methods and theoretical approaches. A new generation of archaeologists was confronted with an enormous body of new information from excavations all over the world. They were trained in the use of new scientific research methods and statistical techniques. They began using computers to store and manipulate large inventories of data. Part of their training was influenced by a new body of theoretical concepts developed by philosophers of science. Not content with description, these scholars began to search for explanations of culture change, for the reasons why societies and cultures evolved in time and space.

These new investigations were spearheaded by archaeologist Lewis Binford, who argued that more rigorous scientific methods were needed to investigate the past. Very explicit scientific investigative methods were now called for. These involved the careful development of research hypotheses that were to be either proved or disproved by scientifically collected data. Binford and his many disciples took archaeology in a new direction. It was not enough just to describe sites, artifacts, life-styles and sequences of human culture. They wanted to understand *why* human cultures were what they were at different stages of prehistoric time all over the world.

This new approach went even further. Instead of assuming that preservation conditions would determine the amount of information that could be obtained about prehistoric societies, Binford and others began by assuming the opposite — that *all* aspects of human cultures and societies, whether material objects or intangibles (like religious beliefs), are preserved (indirectly, perhaps) in archaeological sites, and can be fully recorded. But to recover the more intangible aspects of human society, extremely rigorous methods and precisely formulated research designs were essential. Not only could one recover information about religious and social organization, but one could also develop hypotheses about the very processes that led to changes in human cultures in the past. These hypotheses could be tested against archaeological evidence. Thus, they argued, archaeology is far more than a descriptive subdiscipline of anthropology: it is a science, using scientific methods not only to describe the past, but to explain it as well.

This approach to archaeology is still very much in its infancy, for people are still developing the sophisticated research methods needed to explain culture change in the past. But before we look at culture change, we must examine ways in which archaeologists define *culture*.

2

CULTURE AND THE ARCHAEOLOGICAL RECORD

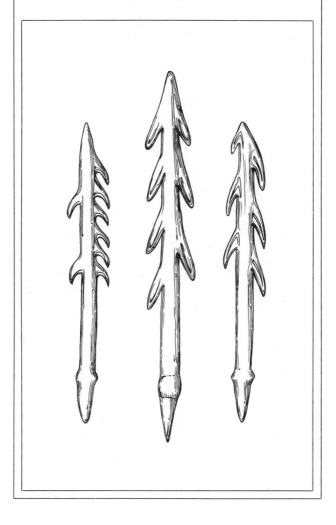

An archaeologist of 6666 A.D. may find himself
obliged to rely on the divergences between assemblages of kitchen utensils to help him recognize that
by 1950, the United Kingdom and United States of
America were not occupied by the same society.

V. GORDON CHILDE, 1956

HUMAN CULTURE

Everyone lives within a cultural context, one that is qualified by a label like "middle-class American," "Roman," or
"Sioux." These labels conjure up certain characteristic objects or behavior patterns typical of this particular culture.
For instance, we associate hamburgers with middle-class
American culture and skin kayaks with Eskimos. Romans are
thought to have spent their time conquering the world,
Sioux wandering over the Great Plains. But our stereotypes
are often crude, inaccurate generalizations. For example, we
think of American Indians as legendary, feathered braves,
but only a few Indian groups ever wore such headdresses. In
fact, the label "American Indian" includes an incredibly
diverse set of peoples, ranging from family size hunter-
gatherer bands to large, complex civilizations.

Each human society has its recognizable cultural style,
which shapes the behavior of its members, their political
and judicial institutions, and their morals. Every traveler is
familiar with the distinctive "flavor" of various cultures
which we experience when dining in a foreign restaurant or
arriving in a strange country. This distinctiveness results
from a people's complex adaptation to a wide range of ecological, societal, and cultural factors.

24

Human culture is unique because much of its content is transmitted from generation to generation by sophisticated communication systems. Formal education, religious beliefs, and day-to-day social intercourse all transmit culture and allow societies to develop complex and ongoing adaptations to aid their survival. Such communication systems also help rapid cultural change to take place, when, for example, less advanced societies come into contact with more advanced ones. Culture is a potential guide for our behavior created through generations of human experience. It provides a design for living that helps mold our responses to different situations.

We humans are the only animals to use our culture as the primary means of adapting to our environment. While biological evolution, for example, has protected the polar bear from arctic winters, only humans make thick clothes and snow igloos in the Arctic and live in light, thatched shelters in the tropics. Culture is an adaptive system; it is a buffer between ourselves, the environment, and other human societies. Through the long millennia of prehistory, human culture has become more elaborate. If this cultural buffer were now removed, we would be helpless and most probably doomed to extinction. As our only means of adaptation, human culture is always adjusting to environmental, technological and societal change.

Culture can be subdivided in many different ways. Language, economics, technology, religion, and political and social organization are but a few of the interacting elements. These elements shape one another and blend to form a whole. For example, the distribution of water and food supplies, as well as flexible social organization, helps determine the distribution of home bases among the San of the Kalahari Desert in southern Africa.

While culture is the dominant factor in determining social behavior, human society is the vehicle that carries our culture. **Societies** are groups of interacting organizers. Insects and other animals, as well as humans, have societies. But only humans have culture as well, a system of habits and customs that we acquire and pass on as our distinctive means of adapting to our environment.

All definitions of culture are theoretical formulations, con-

cepts that are a means of explaining cultures and human behavior in terms of the shared ideas a group of people may
hold. The concept of culture provides anthropological archaeologists with a means to explain the products of human
activity. When archaeologists study the tangible remains of
the past, they see a patterned reflection of the culture that
produced them, of the shared ideas of a group of prehistoric
people. This **patterning** of archaeological finds is critically
important, for it reflects patterned behavior in the past.

CULTURAL SYSTEMS

Many of the interacting components of culture are highly
perishable. So far, no one has been able to dig up a religious
philosophy or an unwritten language. Archaeologists have to
work with the *tangible* remains of human activity that still
survive in the ground. But these surviving remains of human activity are radically affected by *intangible* aspects of human culture. Every copper ornament found in an excavation
is a reflection, not only of the technology that made it, but of
the values and uses which a society placed on such objects.
Ancient tools are not culture in themselves, but they are a
patterned reflection of the culture that produced them. Archaeologists spend much time studying the linkages between past cultures and their archaeological remains.

Anthropologist Leslie White was one of the first to study
peoples' means of adapting to their environment. He argued
that *human culture is made up of many structurally different
parts which articulate with one another within a total cultural
system*. This cultural system is the means whereby a human
society adapts to its physical and social environment.

All cultural systems articulate with other systems, which
also are made up of interacting sets of variables. One such
system is the natural environment. The links between cultural and environmental systems are such that a change in
one system is linked to changes in the other. Thus, a major
objective of archaeology is to understand the linkage between the various parts of cultural and environmental systems as they are reflected in archaeological data. It follows
that archaeologists concerned with cultural systems are more

interested in the *relationships* between different activities and tools within a cultural system than they are in the activities or tools themselves. They are profoundly interested in cultural systems within their environmental context.

To be workable, any human cultural system depends on its ability to adapt to the natural environment. A cultural system can be broken down into all manner of subsystems, religious and ritual subsystems, economic subsystems, and so on. Each of these is linked to the others. Changes in one subsystem, such as a change from cattle herding to wheat growing, will cause reactions in many others. Such relationships concern the archaeologist as a measure of the constant changes and variations in human culture which can accumulate over long periods of time. These changes accumulate as cultural systems respond to external and internal stimuli.

By examining the systematic patternings of archaeological finds, we can find out more about the intangible aspects of human behavior. By dropping their possessions on the ground or burying their dead in certain ways, people have left vital information about many more elements in their cultural system than merely their tools or skeletal remains (Figure 2.1). One can examine the relationships between different individual households by comparing the artifacts left by each; one can study trading practices by analyzing the products of metalsmiths; one can discover religious beliefs through mapping temple architecture. Also, the carefully arranged grave offerings in a royal cemetery tell us much about the ranked members of a royal court buried in a communal grave. And the precise and sophisticated recovery of such data is what modern prehistoric archaeology is all about.

CULTURAL PROCESS

Every cultural system is in a constant state of change. Its various political, social, and technological subsystems adjust to changing circumstances. We ourselves live in a time of rapid cultural change, in which there are measurable differences between different ten-year periods. We would find it hard to identify the thousands of minor, daily, cultural changes that occur, but we can easily recognize the cumula-

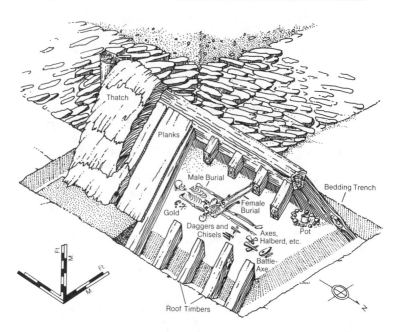

FIGURE 2.1 A wooden burial house from Leubingen, East Germany. The two burials were deposited in a wooden house under a mound. The archaeologist recovers not only the burials, and the objects with which they were buried, but also reconstructs the burial layout and sequence of construction of the burial house. Further, the archaeologist tries to infer the funerary rituals from the artifact patterning and the structures under the mound.

tive effects of these minor changes over a longer period of time.

Consider the many minor changes in automobile design over the past decade, which in themselves are not very striking. But if one looks at the *cumulative* effect of ten years' steady change toward safer cars — energy-absorbing bumpers, padded steering wheels and dashboards, seat belts, many fewer projecting ornaments — the change is very striking. The automobile of today is different from that of the 1960s, and many of the changes are due to tighter governmental safety regulations, which in turn are due to greater public safety consciousness. Here we see a major cumulative change in part of our enormous technological subsystem. By examining the relationship between technological and political subsystems, as in the example above, we can understand the processes by which culture changed.

The word *process* implies a patterned sequence of events, one event leading to another. A three-bedroom house is built in an ordered sequence of events, from foundation footings up to final painting. (Archaeological research itself has a process — research design and formulating hypotheses; collecting, and interpreting, data to test those hypotheses; publishing the results.) To analyze cultural process, we consider all the factors which cause changes in human culture and how they affect one another.

How did human cultures change in the past? What cultural processes came into play when people began to cultivate the soil, or when complex and elaborate urban states developed five thousand years ago? As we saw in Chapter 1, at first students of the past thought that major inventions like agriculture had been invented by a single genius. The new discoveries were thought to have spread throughout the world by mass migrations, or by long-distance trading over continents and oceans. But as more and more archaeological data have accumulated in all corners of the world, people have realized that such straightforward explanations of cultural process as universal evolution, or the spread of all ideas from a single place of invention, are far too simplistic to reflect actual reality.

Most changes in human culture have been cumulative, occurring slowly, over a long time. Processes of culture change in prehistory were the result of constantly changing adaptations to a myriad of different external environments. Cultural systems were constantly adjusting and evolving in response to feedback from both inside and outside.

Clearly, no one element in a cultural system is a primary cause of culture change, because a complex range of different factors — rainfall, vegetation, technology, social restrictions, and population density, to mention only a few — interact with one another and react to a change in any element in the system. Human culture is, therefore, from the ecologist's point of view, merely one element in the ecosystem, a mechanism of behavior whereby people adapt to this environment. This viewpoint provides a useful framework for much modern archaeological research, and for studying cultural process.

We shall look more closely at ways in which people have sought to interpret cultural process in prehistory in Chapter 7.

THE ARCHAEOLOGICAL RECORD

Prehistoric archaeologists study ancient human behavior by way of the surviving traces of such behavior in food remains, structures, and humanly manufactured objects. These material remains form the **archaeological record,** the archives of human history before written records.

The archaeological record consists of all kinds of archaeological finds, from the pyramids of Gizeh to an early human campsite at Olduvai Gorge, Tanzania, occupied nearly two million years ago. California shell mounds, Ohio earthworks, Inca cemeteries, all are part of the archaeological record. So are isolated artifacts — the throne of Tutankhamun, a wooden religious mask from a midwestern burial mound, or a Polynesian stone adze.

We seek to find out about prehistoric people from the traces of their activities. The butchered carcass of a mammoth slaughtered twenty thousand years ago is a mine of information on ancient hunting practices. Analysis of dried-out seeds or ancient human body waste found in archaeological sites tell us much about prehistoric diet.

What we can find out about the past is severely limited, it is true, by the state of preservation of archaeological finds. Some substances like baked clay or stone will survive indefinitely. But wood, bone, leather, and other organic materials soon vanish except under waterlogged or exceptionally dry conditions. Everyone has heard of the remarkable tomb of Egyptian pharaoh Tutankhamun ("King Tut"), whose astonishing treasure survived almost intact in the dry climate of the Nile Valley for more than three thousand years (Figure 2.2). In this case, the archaeological record is exceptionally complete and informative. We even know, for example, from the bouquet of wildflowers laid on his inner coffin, that Tutankhamun's funeral took place in the spring.

FIGURE 2.2 The throne of Tutankhamun, one of the many wooden artifacts recovered from the richest royal sepulchre ever found.

But most archaeological sites are found where only a few durable materials survive. Constructing the past from these finds is a challenge, the sort of problem faced by the detective piecing together the circumstances of a crime from a few fragmentary clues. The analogy is an apt one. Take, for example, two spark plugs, a fragment of a china cup, a needle, a grindstone, and a candlestick. Imagine someone from Patagonia digging them up in a thousand years' time and trying to tell you how the makers *used* the objects. This is precisely what the archaeologist does in going about the work of being a special type of anthropologist.

The data we amass from **survey** (looking for sites) and **excavation** (digging) make up the archaeological record. The two basic units studied by archaeologists are **sites** and **artifacts**.

Archaeological Sites

Archaeology is based on the scientific recovery of data from the ground, on the systematic excavation and recording of the archaeological record. The **archaeological site** is a place where traces of ancient human activity are to be found. It is the archaeologist's archive, much in the same way that a set of government files can represent the day-by-day record of historical events. Sites are normally identified through the presence of humanly manufactured tools, or artifacts, found in them.

Archaeological sites can range in size from a huge prehistoric city like Teotihuacán, in the Valley of Mexico, to a small campsite occupied by hunter-gatherers at Olduvai Gorge, Tanzania. An archaeological site can consist of a single human burial, a huge rockshelter occupied over thousands of years, or a simple scatter of stone tools found on the surface at the bottom of Death Valley, California. Sites are limited in number and variety by preservation conditions and by the nature of the activities of the people who occupied them. Some were used for a few short hours, others for a generation or two. Some, like Mesopotamian city mounds, were important settlements for hundreds, even thousands, of years and contain many separate occupation layers. Great mounds like that of Ur-of-the-Chaldees in Mesopotamia contain many occupation levels, which tell the story of a long-established, ancient city that was abandoned when the river Euphrates changed its course away from the settlement.

Archaeological sites are most commonly classified according to the activities that occurred there. Thus, cemeteries and other sepulchres like Tutankhamun's tomb are referred to as **burial sites.** An Olduvai campsite with remains of game butchery and of crude shelters and domestic activities is a **habitation site.** So are many other sites, such as caves and rockshelters, early Mesoamerican farming villages, and Mesopotamian cities — all of them places where people lived and carried out a wide range of different activities. **Kill sites** consist of bones of slaughtered game animals and the weapons which killed them. They are found in East Africa and on the North American Great Plains. **Quarry sites** are another type of specialist site, where people mined stone or metals to make specific tools. Certain prized raw materials, such as obsidian, a volcanic glass used for fine knives, were widely traded in prehistoric times and are of considerable interest to the archaeologist. Then there are archaeology's spectacular **religious sites,** like the famous stone circles of Stonehenge in southern England, the Temple of Amun at Karnak, Egypt, and the great ceremonial centers of the lowland Maya in Mexico, such as Tikal, Copán, and Palenque (Figure 2.3). **Art sites** are commonplace in southwestern France, southern Africa, and parts of North America, places where prehistoric people painted or engraved magnificent displays of art (see Figure 8.4). Some French art sites are at least fifteen thousand years old.

Each of these site types represents a particular form of human activity, one that is represented in the archaeological record by specific artifact patterns and surface indications found and recorded by the archaeologist.

Artifacts

Artifacts are objects found in archaeological sites that exhibit features which are the result of human activity. The term *artifact* covers every form of archaeological find, from stone axes to gold ornaments, houses, and other structures, as well as food remains such as broken bones. What distinguishes artifacts from nonartifacts is simply that artifacts display patterns of humanly caused features, or attributes. These objects can be classified according to the distinctive attributes they display. Artifacts are the product of human ideas, ideas which people had about the way certain objects should look. Every culture has its own rules, which limit and dicate the form of artifacts. Our own society has definite ideas of what a fork should look like, or a motor car, or a pair of shoes. We are familiar with the artifacts of other cultures, so much so that we can see, for example, a skin kayak, and identify it as "Eskimo" at once.

The idea of how an object should look is primarily established in the mind of its maker. He or she manipulates the raw material, let it be stone, clay, metal, or some other substance, to produce an artifact that coincides with his or her

FIGURE 2.3   Temple I at Tikal, Guatemala, dating to about A.D. 700, an example of part of a religious site.

mental template of what such an object should look like. The form of the resulting artifact closely approximates this template. The variations in a group of similar objects, such as stone projectile points, reflect variations in the ideas behind them. Archaeologists study and classify artifacts, as we discuss in Chapter 7. These classifications are really research devices, means by which archaeologists study the products of human behavior and, indirectly, human behavior itself. But what ultimately creates the mental templates that give form to our artifacts?

Most craft skills, like stone toolmaking, pottery manufacture, basketry, or metallurgy, are learned by each new generation. The skills are transmitted from one generation to the next, and the mental templates of what an axe should look like are perpetuated for hundreds, even thousands, of years. Tradition, then, plays an important role in the creation of artifact forms.

Every artifact possesses a number of **attributes,** identifiable features which combine to give the object its distinctive form. The pot illustrated in Figure 2.4 has several obvious attributes: an out-turned lip, a band of decoration on the neck, a rounded base, and so on. Each of these attributes contributes to the form of the pot and was part of the mental template that produced it. Each attribute has a different reason for being there. The band of decoration is purely ornamental, part of the decorative tradition of the people who made it. The shape of the pot is determined by its function. It was designed for carrying liquids and for cooking, and a bag-shaped, round-bottomed body is essential for these purposes. Attributes can be present because of traditional, functional, technological, or other reasons. Just occasionally a new attribute will appear, a new decorative motif perhaps, that will vanish just as fast as it appeared. Why? Because it did not catch on with other potmakers and never became part of the communal mental template. Just occasionally, too, a new attribute may achieve widespread popularity and be adopted by everyone. Then the mental template of the makers changes a little and the innovation becomes part of the pottery tradition. But the mental templates that govern the "correct" forms of pots among neighboring peoples may be completely different.

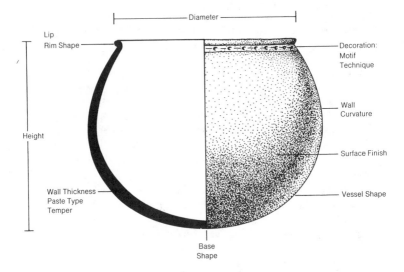

FIGURE 2.4 Attributes on a clay pot. "Each of these attributes contributes to the form of the pot and was part of the mental template that produced it."

The archaeologist is deeply concerned with how artifacts vary and with the changing forms of the many manufactured objects found in archaeological sites. Variation in the form of artifacts is a complex subject, but one of critical importance to archaeologists. It is the cumulative results of thousands of minor changes in the mental templates of dozens of different artifacts that provide the tangible evidence for culture change in the prehistoric past. And that, as we have seen, is a major concern of anyone studying world prehistory.

CONTEXT

Artifacts are found in archaeological sites. Archaeological sites are far more than just a collection of artifacts, however. They can contain the remains of dwellings, burials, storage pits, craft activities, and sometimes several occupation levels. Each artifact, each broken bone or tiny seed, every dwelling, has a relationship in space and time to all the other finds made in the site. An artifact can be earlier, contemporary with, or later than its neighbors in the soil. A thousand obsidian flakes and half-completed projectile heads scattered over an area several square feet in diameter are, in themselves, merely stone fragments. But the patterning of all the fragments is significant, as it tells us something of the various manufacturing activities carried out by the person who flaked the thousand fragments from several chunks of obsidian. In this instance, and many others, the **context** of the artifacts in time and space is vital.

To every archaeologist, an artifact is worthless without this context. The museums and art galleries of the world are filled with magnificent artifacts that have been collected under circumstances that can only be described as highly unscientific. Generations of treasure hunters have ravaged ancient Egyptian cemeteries and dug up thousands of pre-Columbian pots for museums and private collectors. Few of these objects have any archaeological context. Any expert can look at a pre-Columbian pot and say at once, "Classic Maya." But, tragically, it is only in rare cases that our expert will be able to consult excavation records and say, "Classic Maya, Level VIB from Temple of the Inscriptions, Palenque, excavation C, 1976, associated with burial of an adult male, thirty-five years old, date about A.D. 680." An artifact removed from its context in space and time in an archaeological site is merely an object. An artifact carefully excavated from a recorded archaeological context is an integral part of our history, and as such, has far more significance. This context of space and time lies at the very foundations of modern archaeology. We must now look at ways in which we tell how old something is, and what its spatial associations may be.

3

TIME

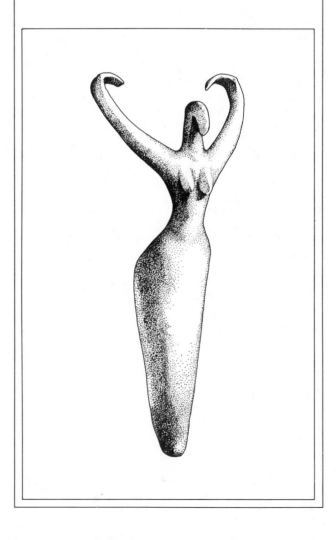

> What seest thou else in the dark backward and
> abysm of time?
>
> WILLIAM SHAKESPEARE, *The Tempest*

This chapter is about time, about the ways in which archaeologists date projectile points and all the other myriad finds that come from their excavations and surveys.

Human prehistory spans at least four million years of human cultural evolution, a vast landscape of sites peopled with long-abandoned food remains, artifacts, burials, and prehistoric dwellings. Each of these sites and their contents has a precise context in time, an exact position in space as well. Some sites, like the great city of Teotihuacán in Mexico, were occupied for hundreds of years. Other localities, such as Olduvai Gorge, were inhabited for thousands. The chronology of prehistory world-wide is made up from thousands of careful excavations and a wide variety of dating tests, used to develop hundreds of local sequences of occupation layers and archaeological sites. Without dates, prehistory would be a jumble of confusing sites and cultures without order.

Our lives are governed by time — by working hours and tax deadlines, bus schedules and precise calendars. Everyone in our society needs access to a timepiece, simply to keep up with everyone else. Precise time measurement is, however, a recent phenomenon. Accurate historical records extend back only five thousand years, to the beginning of ancient Egyptian and Mesopotamian civilizations. Both these societies developed calendars and astronomical predictions to a fine

39

art. The Maya peoples of Mesoamerica developed an astronomically based calendar which they used to precisely regulate cycles of years upon which the prosperity of society depended.

Looking earlier than 3000 B.C., however, we enter a chronological vacuum, a blank that archaeologists have labored to fill with carefully developed sequences of sites and artifacts. Despite all efforts, prehistoric time must be measured in centuries and millennia, rather than individual years. We know that Washington, D.C. was founded in A.D. 1800. We will be lucky if we can ever date the beginnings of Teotihuacán to closer than 200 ± 100 B.C. years. Some idea of the scale of the problem can be gained by piling up a hundred quarters. If the entire pile represents the time that humankind has been on earth, the length of time covered by historical records would be considerably less than the thickness of one quarter. Ninety-nine and nine-tenths percent of all human experience lies in prehistoric times. Small wonder time is important in archaeology.

RELATIVE CHRONOLOGY

Every event or object has a time relationship to other events and objects. If I place a book on a table, and then pile another one on top of it, clearly the upper one of the two was placed on the table after — at a later moment in time than — the original volume. The second book became part of the pile after the first, but how long afterward we have no means of telling. This example illustrates the principle of superposition, the cornerstone of **relative chronology.**

Superposition, the notion that underlying levels are earlier than those that cover them, came to archaeology from geology. The geological layers of the earth are superimposed one upon another almost like layers of a cake. Easily viewed examples are cliffs by the seashore or road cuts along the highway, which show a series of geological levels. Obviously, any object deposited in the lower horizons got there before the upper strata were accumulated. In other words, the lower levels are relatively earlier than the later strata. The deposition of a series of occupation levels or geological strata in order can be achieved by many different processes, by wind, water, earthquakes, and other factors.

Superposition is fundamental to the study of archaeological sites, for many settlements, like desert caves in western North America, or Near Eastern mounds, were occupied more or less continuously for hundreds, even thousands, of years. Human occupation of any site results in the accumulation of all kinds of rubbish. Objects are lost and become imbedded in the soil. Buildings fall into disrepair and are leveled to make way for new ones. A flood may wipe out a village and deposit a thick layer of clay. A new village may rise on the same spot years later. The sequence of these superimposed occupation levels is carefully recorded as the excavation of a site proceeds. Of course, not all settlements were occupied several times. Single-occupation sites, even very temporary camps, are studied just as carefully.

The sequence of natural and humanly accumulated layers on an archaeological site is the basis for all stratigraphic observations in archaeology. But as Figure 3.1 shows, it is not only the carefully observed layers, but their detailed contents as well, that provide us with relative chronology. Each level in a settlement has its associated artifacts, objects that the archaeologist uses as indicators of technological, economic, social, or even religious change.

Artifacts and Relative Chronology

Manufactured artifacts are the fundamental data archaeologists use to study past human behavior. These artifacts have changed through time in radical ways. One only has to look at the humble stone chopper of the earliest humans and compare it with the latest electric carving knife to get the point. Most artifact changes in prehistory are extremely small; minor changes in such things as the shape, decoration, or lip angle of clay pots accumulate slowly over time as they ultimately lead to a vessel form that is hardly recognizable as originating from its ancestors.

Archaeologists, like the celebrated Egyptologist Flinders Petrie, have long been fascinated by the gradual evolution of artifacts. Petrie, who worked on a huge prehistoric cemetery

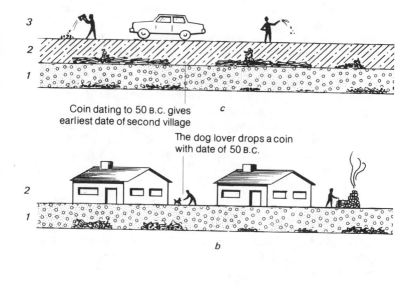

Coin dating to 50 B.C. gives
earliest date of second village

c

The dog lover drops a coin
with date of 50 B.C.

b

a

FIGURE 3.1 The principle of superposition. (a) A farming village built on virgin subsoil. After a time, the village is abandoned and the huts fall into disrepair. Their ruins are covered by accumulating soil and vegetation. (b) After an interval, a second village is built on the same site, with different architectural styles. This in turn is abandoned; the houses collapse into piles of rubble and are covered by accumulating soil. (c) Twentieth-century people park their cars on top of both village sites and drop litter and coins which, when uncovered, reveal to the archaeologist that the top layer is modern.

An archaeologist digging this site would find that the modern layer is underlain by two prehistoric occupation levels, that square houses were in use in the upper of the two, which is the later (law of superposition), and that round huts are stratigraphically earlier than square ones here. Therefore, village 1 is earlier than village 2, but when either was occupied or how many years separate village 1 from 2 cannot be known without further data.

at Diospolis Parva, Egypt, in 1902, was confronted with the problem of arranging a large number of tombs in chronological order. He eventually placed them in sequence by studying the groups of pots buried with each skeleton, arranging the vessels in such a way that features like handle design reflected gradual change. The earliest handles were useful for lifting the pot. But the latest vessels bore no handles at all, merely some painted lines that represented the once useful handle. Petrie used his pots to create a series of "sequence dates," each of them characterized by a certain vessel form. Whenever a vessel form similar to Petrie's was found anywhere in Egypt, the pot itself and the objects found with it could be dated within his series. So effective was this relative chronology based on artifacts that it was used for many years.

Recent studies of changing artifacts are based on the assumption that the popularity of any artifact is a fleeting thing. The miniskirt becomes the midi or the maxi; clothing styles change from month to month. Records hit the Top Forty but are forgotten within a short time. Other artifacts have a far longer life. The stone choppers of the earliest humans were a major element in early toolkits (a toolkit is a basic set of tools used by a culture) for hundreds of thousands of years. People used candles for centuries before they turned to kerosine and gas lamps. But each has its period of maximum popularity, or frequency of occurrence, whether this lasts for millennia or only a few months. Figure 3.2 shows how each distribution of artifacts, when plotted, has a profile that has been described as resembling a large battleship's hull viewed from above.

The relatively unsophisticated methods used by Flinders Petrie have been refined into sophisticated **seriation** (ordering) **techniques.** They are based on the assumption that the popularity of certain pottery types, stone artifact forms, and other objects peak in the "battleship curve." Thus, it is argued, sites within a restricted geographic area which contain similar pottery and other artifact types are of approximately the same relative date. If the samples are statistically reliable, a series of sites can be linked in a relative chronology, even though, without dates in years, one cannot tell when they were occupied.

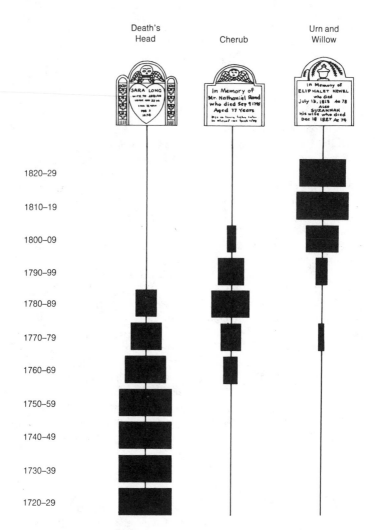

FIGURE 3.2 Seriation. The changing styles of New England grave-stones from Stoneham, Massachusetts, between 1720 and 1829, ser-iated in three different styles. Notice how each style rises to a peak of maximum popularity and then declines as another comes into fashion. The cherub style shows the "classic battleship curve."

Edwin Dethlefsen and James Deetz tested this "battleship curve" assumption against the changing decorative styles on gravestones in New England Colonial cemeteries. They found that the changing styles of death's heads, cherubs, and urns succeeded one another in an almost perfect series of battleship curves. In this case, the dates of the gravestones were known from their inscriptions, so the experiment could be conducted and tested within a precise chronological context.

A series of archaeological sites may contain many different artifacts that appear and vanish over relatively short periods of time. By using seriation, it is possible to place the different forms of artifacts in a series of relative chronologies, like that from the Tehuacán Valley in Mexico illustrated in Figure 3.3. Each occupation level of each site will contain different proportions of each artifact form manufactured at that particular period. And once a sequence of changing artifact frequencies has been developed, it is possible to fit isolated, newly discovered sites into your relative chronology.

Cross Dating

Seriation is effective for **cross dating** sites as well. As we have seen, it can be used to assign a newly discovered settlement to a precise position in the relative chronology of a well-studied area, as Flinders Petrie did. In some cases, too, a series of sites may contain objects such as European coins whose date of minting is known. Hence, we have access to dates in years. A treasured coin traded into the village from far away falls on a hut floor and is lost. Centuries later, the archaeologists find the dated coin in this prehistoric Indian site and know it was traded for goods *no earlier than its date of minting*. They may find more sites with the same Indian pottery types in similar proportions — but no coins — a few miles away. When they seriate the finds, they will be able to cross date the undated settlements, because their artifact frequencies are the same. This cross dating technique has been widely applied to central European prehistoric sites, whose inhabitants traded with literate civilizations in the Mediterranean basin, exchanging copper and other raw materials for ornaments and other luxuries whose age in years is known.

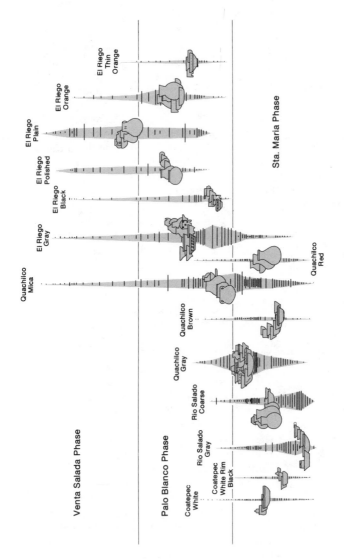

FIGURE 3.3 Seriation of pottery styles from the Tehuacán Valley, Mexico, showing many sites ordered into a single sequence.

Relative Chronology and the Ice Age

The story of human prehistory has unfolded against a backdrop of massive and startling climatic changes (Figure 3.4). The "Ice Age" or **Pleistocene** is the most recent of the great geological epochs, commonly known as the "Age of Humanity." On at least four occasions during the Pleistocene, great ice sheets covered much of western Europe and North America, bringing arctic climate to vast areas of the northern hemisphere (Figure 3.4b). These glacial periods were separated by prolonged periods of much warmer climate when the ice sheets retreated to northern latitudes. Traces of human settlement are commonplace in Europe after four hundred thousand years ago, remains of hunter-gatherers' camp sites that once flourished by great rivers like the Thames. Thousands of stone tools have come from Thames gravels, artifacts that were manufactured during warmer periods when such animals as the hippopotamus lived in northern Europe.

Geologists are still trying to puzzle out the complicated sequence of warm and cold periods during the Pleistocene. But we do know that the last glaciation affected Europe and North America between about seventy thousand and ten thousand years ago. It was during this period that *Homo sapiens* first emerged, that people first settled in the Americas, and that the first artistic traditions developed in French caves.

The framework of glaciations and warmer periods provides only a very general chronology for prehistory. Relatively few prehistoric peoples lived on or very near the great ice sheets. But their campsites have been discovered on the shores of long-dried up Pleistocene lakes that were later sealed by the subsequent movement of advancing ice sheets. The dried-up deposits of these lakes are rich in organic materials that provide a wealth of information on the environment at the time the site was occupied. Millions of tiny fossil pollen grains from the trees and undergrowth that once grew near the lake are preserved in the lake filling. These pollen grains are highly distinctive and readily identified, since each tree species, even each kind of grass, has a different form. By taking samples from the lake deposits, it is possible

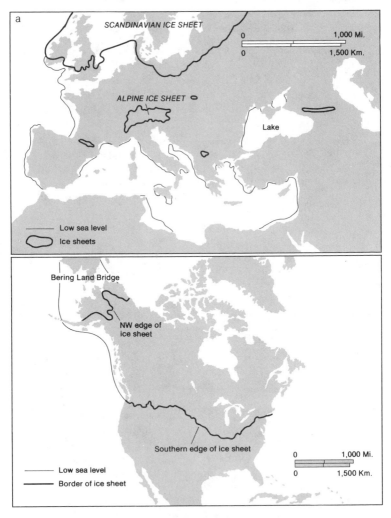

FIGURE 3.4 Pleistocene relative chronology. (a) The distribution of the major ice sheets in Europe and North America during the last glaciation of the Pleistocene, and the extent of land exposed by low sea levels; (b) The framework of glacial periods during the Pleistocene; (c) The surroundings of a hunter-gatherer camp from northern England, occupied about 10,000 years ago, reconstructed by pollen analysis.

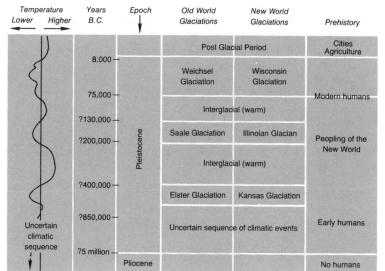

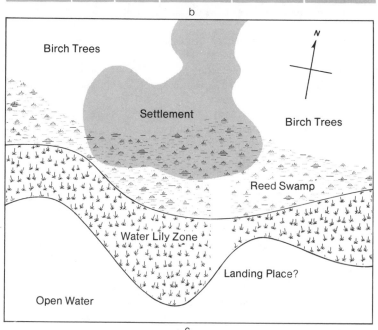

to reconstruct the vegetation of a Pleistocene lake by counting and identifying the fossil pollens.

This technique is **palynology,** the science of pollen analysis, about the only means of obtaining an accurate picture of prehistoric environments in any detail. Pollen samples have shown how African hunter-gatherers living in central Africa fifty thousand years ago were exploiting dense rainforests. In 10,000 B.C., present western Europe was covered with treeless arctic plains swept by icy winds. It has taken only a few thousand years for northern Europe to change from arctic climate to the temperate environment of today. Minute changes in vegetational cover accompanied these climatic shifts, changes that can be traced by studying pollens of the lake clays and muds in which many archaeological sites lie (Figure 3.4c), and each vegetation type can be assigned to a dated zone of post-Pleistocene time.

The Pleistocene also witnessed major changes in world sea levels. During glacial periods sea levels fell by several hundred feet, as water became locked up in huge ice sheets. When warmer climates returned, sea levels rose again. Some ancient high sea levels can be seen above the modern coastline. Sometimes prehistoric settlements are found on such high beaches, occupied when the oceans were more extensive than today. The geological date of the abandoned beach tells you the date of the site on it.

These sea level changes radically altered world geography (Figure 3.4a). During periods of low sea level, people could walk across the Bering Strait from Asia to North America, and could hunt dry-shod over what is now the English Channel and the North Sea. Thousands of archaeological sites are buried under the oceans, settlements that have the potential, for example, to tell us when people first entered North America. Rising sea levels tended to isolate human populations, and, like other climatic fluctuations, to encourage human adaption to a wider variety of different environments than ever before. Without question, the present diversity of humankind can, in part, be attributed to the constant shifts in world climate over the past four million years.

The relative chronology of the Pleistocene provides a general framework for the major events of prehistory. This framework becomes much more accurate after seventy thousand years B.C., when many more sites are found near lakes and other localities where pollen analysis can be used to study vegetational and environmental changes.

DATING IN YEARS (CHRONOMETRIC DATING)

People have tried everything to date the past in calendar years. Today, a whole battery of such **chronometric,** or absolute, dating methods are available to the archaeologist. Some are reliable, well-tried techniques, like tree-ring dating and potassium argon dating. Others are most experimental, like amino acid racemization, obsidian hydration, and thermoluminescence. We do not have the space to discuss all these methods here, so we shall confine ourselves to the more widely used chronometric techniques. Fortunately, these straddle most of prehistoric times (Figure 3.5). Readers interested in more experimental methods should consult the "Further Reading" section at the end of the book.

Historical Records and Objects of Known Age

In the Near East, five thousand years of history are recorded in government archives, on inscriptions, and on thousands of clay tablets. As we saw in Chapter 1, archaeology provides us with a means of checking and expanding historical records. But the lists of kings and genealogies in early Egyptian and Mesopotamian archives provide us with dates in years that go back to at least 3000 B.C. Recorded history starts in about 750 B.C. in the central Mediterranean, about 55 B.C. in Britain. The first historical records for the New World began with the Spanish Conquest, while parts of Africa entered "history" in A.D. 1890. Historical records cover but the very smallest fraction of the human experience.

Fortunately, the literate civilizations of three or four thousand years ago traded their products far and wide. The Egyptians traded fine ornaments to Crete, the Cretans sent wine and fine pottery to the Nile. When archaeologist Arthur Evans discovered the magnificent Minoan civilization of Crete in 1900, he dated the Palace of Knossos by means of

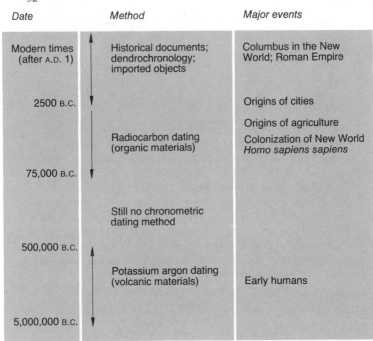

Date	Method	Major events
Modern times (after A.D. 1)	Historical documents; dendrochronology; imported objects	Columbus in the New World; Roman Empire
2500 B.C.		Origins of cities
		Origins of agriculture
	Radiocarbon dating (organic materials)	Colonization of New World *Homo sapiens sapiens*
75,000 B.C.		
	Still no chronometric dating method	
500,000 B.C.		
	Potassium argon dating (volcanic materials)	Early humans
5,000,000 B.C.		

FIGURE 3.5   Major chronological methods in prehistory.

Minoan pottery fragments which had been excavated in faraway Egypt, in levels whose precise historical date was known. Coins and other imports of known age can be used to date buildings or refuse pits in which they were dropped centuries earlier. A bewildering array of dated objects are used by archaeologists dealing with the recent periods of prehistory. These include glass bottles and beads, seals, imported Chinese porcelain, even military buttons. Each of these objects has the advantage that it is of exact known age.

Tree-ring Dating (Dendrochronology)

Everyone is familiar with the concentric growth rings that can be seen in the cross section of a felled tree trunk. These rings are formed in most trees, and they are of special importance to archaeologists in areas like the American Southwest, where there is a marked seasonal weather change and growth is concentrated in a few months of the year. Normally trees produce one growth ring a year, which is formed by the cambium between the wood and the bark. Each year's growth forms a distinct ring that varies in thickness according to the tree's age and annual climatic variations. Weather variations in the Southwest tend to run in cycles of dry and wet years, which are reflected in patterns of thicker and thinner rings on the trees.

The tree-ring samples are taken with a borer from living or felled trees. The ring sequences from the borer are then compared to each other and to a master chronology of rings built up from many different trees with overlapping sequences. The patterns of thick and thin rings for the new sequences are matched to the master sequence and are dated on the basis of their accurate fit to the master sequence. By using the California bristlecone pine, tree-ring experts have developed a master chronology over eight thousand years back into the past.

Tree-ring dating can be practiced on long-felled wooden beams from Indian pueblos to date the buildings of which they are a part. Tree-ring experts have been able to develop an extremely accurate chronology for southwestern sites that extend back as long ago as 59 B.C. It was a difficult task, for they had to connect a prehistoric chronology from dozens of ancient beams to a master tree-ring chronology connected to modern times obtained from living trees of known age. The dates of such famous southwestern sites as Mesa Verde and Pueblo Bonito are known to within a few years.

Dendrochronology has been used in other areas of the world as well, in Alaska, the Mississippi Valley, and in Germany. Living Irish oaks have been dated back to A.D. 1649, and farmhouse and church beams have taken Ireland's chronologies back to A.D. 1380. Oak beams in the Speyer and Trier cathedrals in Germany go back to A.D. 383, while Celtic and Roman beams extend from about 700 B.C. to A.D. 339. These two chronologies have been joined to form tree-ring sequence going back some 2,700 years. Dutch tree-ring experts have even used the oak panels utilized by painting masters to date and authenticate their works of art!

Unfortunately, tree-ring dating can be used only on rela-

tively recent settlements in restricted regions of markedly
seasonal rainrall. But, as we shall see, dendrochronology is
also useful for calibrating radiocarbon dates.

Radiocarbon Dating

Radiocarbon dating, developed by physicists J. R. Arnold
and W. F. Libby in 1949, is the best known of all chronometric
methods. Cosmic radiation produces neutrons that enter the
earth's atmosphere and react with nitrogen to produce the
carbon isotope carbon 14 (C14, or radiocarbon), which contains fourteen rather than the usual twelve neutrons in its
nucleus. With these additional neutrons, the nucleus is un-
stable and is subject to radioactive decay. Arnold and Libby
calculated that it took 5,568 years for half of the C14 in any
sample to decay, the so-called half-life of C14.

Carbon 14 is believed to behave just like ordinary carbon
(C12) from a chemical standpoint. Together with C12 it enters
into the carbon dioxide of the atmosphere, in which a varying
amount of C14 is to be found. Since living vegetation builds
up its own organic matter by photosynthesis and by using
atmospheric carbon dioxide, the ratio of C14 to C12 in living
vegetation is equal to that in the atmosphere. The very short
lifetime of individual plants is negligible compared with the
half-life of radiocarbon. As soon as an organism dies, no
further radiocarbon is incorporated into it. The radiocarbon
present in the dead organism will continue to disintegrate so
that after 5,568 years half the original amount will be left; after
about 11,100 years, a quarter; and so on. Thus, measurement
of the amount of C14 still present and emitting radiation in
plant and animal remains enables us to determine the time
that has elapsed since their death. By calculating the difference between the amount of C14 originally present and that
now present, and comparing the difference with the known
rate of decay, we can compute the time elapsed in years. The
amount of C14 present in a fresh sample emits beta particles at
a rate of about fifteen particles per minute per gram of carbon.
A sample with an emission rate of half that amount would be
approximately 5,568 years old, the time needed for one-half
the original radioactive material to disintegrate (the half-life
of C14).

Radiocarbon samples can be taken from a wide range of organic materials. About a handful of charcoal, burnt bone, shell, hair, wood, or other organic substance is needed for the laboratory. This means that few actual artifacts may be dated, for wooden and other organic artifacts are rare. But charcoal from hearths is frequently used for dating. The samples themselves are collected with meticulous care from impeccable stratigraphic contexts so that an exact location, or a specific structure, is dated.

The laboratory converts the sample to gas and pumps it into a proportional counter. The beta particle emissions are measured, usually for a period of twenty-four hours. The results of the count are then converted to an age determination. When a C14 date comes from a laboratory, it bears a statistical plus or minus factor. For example, 3600 ± 200 years (200 years represents one standard deviation) means that chances are two out of three that the correct date is between the span of 3,400 and 3,800. If we double the deviation, chances are nineteen out of twenty that the span 3,200 to 4,000 is correct. So radiocarbon dates should be recognized for what they are — statistical approximations.

When J. R. Arnold and W. F. Libby first developed radiocarbon dating, they compared their C14 readings with dates obtained from objects of known age, such as ancient Egyptian boats. These tests enabled them to claim that radiocarbon dates were accurate enough for archaeologists' purposes. But just when archaeologists thought they had at last been presented with an accurate and reliable means of dating the past, some radiocarbon dates for dated tree rings of long-lived California bristlecone pines were published. They turned out to be consistently younger—for trees dating to before 1200 B.C.

It turned out that Libby had made an incorrect assumption. He had argued that the concentration of radiocarbon in living things has remained constant through time, so that prehistoric samples, when they were alive, would have contained the same amount of radiocarbon as living things today. But, in fact, changes in the strength of the earth's magnetic field and alternations in solar activity have considerably varied the concentration of radiocarbon in the atmosphere and in living things.

Fortunately, however, it is possible to correct C14 dates back to about 4500 B.C. by calibrating them with tree-ring chronologies, for dendrochronology provides absolutely precise dates. Some idea of the changes in accuracy of C14 dating over the past six thousand years can be obtained from Figure 3.6. Calibration of dates earlier than 4500 B.C. is impossible because tree-ring chronologies are lacking, but extreme accuracy is less important for earlier periods anyway because time scales are less precise.

Despite its chronological and technical limitations, radiocarbon dating is of enormous significance to archaeology. C14 samples have dated some African hunter-gatherers to over fifty thousand years ago and Paleo-Indian bison kills on the Great Plains to over eight thousand years before the present, and they have provided chronologies for the origins of agriculture and civilization in the New and Old World. Radiocarbon dates provide a means of developing a truly global chronology, one that can equate major events such as

FIGURE 3.6 The difference between C14 dates and actual dates in years from 4500 B.C. to modern times.

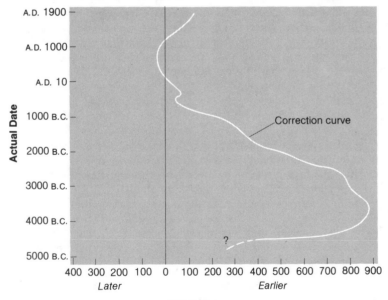

C14 Dating

the origin of literate civilizations in such widely separated areas as China and Peru. The prehistory of the world from some seventy-five thousand years ago up to historic times is dated almost entirely by the radiocarbon method.

Early Prehistory

Earlier than seventy-five thousand years ago, we enter a long period of prehistory that is essentially undated. Some experimental dating methods such as **fission track dating,** a technique based on the fission decay rate of uranium atoms in minerals, are being developed to fill this gap. But their archaeological applications are still very limited, and the reader should consult the references in "Further Reading" for a description of this and other experimental techniques.

The period between seventy-five thousand and five hundred thousand years ago was one of slow human cultural evolution, when *Homo sapiens* first appear in the archaeological record. At present, we have no idea exactly when, or how, modern humans first evolved. Obviously, such information must await the development of new dating methods and the discovery of additional archaeological sites.

Potassium Argon Dating

Archaeological sites earlier than about half a million years old can be dated by a radioactive counting technique known as **potassium argon dating.** Geologists use this method to date rocks as early as four to five billion years ago and as recent as four hundred thousand years before the present. Potassium (K) is one of the most abundant elements in the earth's crust and is present in nearly every mineral. In its natural form, potassium contains a small proportion of radioactive ^{40}K atoms. For every one hundred ^{40}K atoms that decay, 11 percent become argon 40, an inactive gas that can easily escape from its present material by diffusion when lava and other molten rocks are formed. As volcanic rocks form by crystallization, the concentration of argon 40 drops to almost nothing. But the process of decay over time of ^{40}K continues, and 11 percent of every one hundred ^{40}K atoms will become argon 40. So, it is possible to measure the concentration of argon 40 that has accumulated since the rock formed, using a spectrometer.

Many archaeological sites, such as the campsites at Olduvai Gorge, Tanzania, were formed during periods of intense
volcanic activity. Dates have been obtained for contemporary
lava flows, sometimes stratified above and below campsites
of early humans. The inhabitants of these sites picked up
lava fragments and fashioned them into tools, which can be
dated. Louis and Mary Leakey were able to obtain potassium
argon dates for campsites at Olduvai where early human fossils were found. The samples gave readings of about 1.75
million years.

Even earlier dates have come from sites at Hadar in Ethiopia
and on the eastern shores of Lake Turkana in northern Kenya,
where fragments of early humans have been dated by potassium argon techniques using contemporary lavas to over two
million years ago. Chopper tools of undoubted human manufacture have come from Koobi Fora in northern Kenya, dated
to about 1.85 million years, still the earliest date for human
toolmaking yet recorded.

Like C14, potassium argon dates have a large standard deviation, in the order of 0.25 million years for early Pleistocene sites. On the other hand, some of the world's most important early archaeological sites are found in volcanically
active areas, and, as a result, we are fortunate in having at
least a provisional chronology for the earliest chapters of human evolution, one far more accurate than the educated
guesses of earlier generations.

Archaeologists base their studies of time on precise stratigraphic excavations and records and on proven, as well as
experimental, dating techniques. These data and analyses
provide a provisional time scale for world prehistory. Potassium argon dates place human origins at least as early as four
million years, the emergence of *Homo erectus* to about 1.5
million. Radiocarbon dates assign the earliest cave art of
western Europe to earlier than 15,000 B.C., the origins of agriculture in the Near East and also in the Americas to before
8000 B.C. We know that Mesopotamians were living in sizable city-states by 3200 B.C., the Olmec of Mexico flourishing
before 1000 B.C. Tree-ring chronologies date Mesa Verde,
Colorado, to A.D. 1150, and historical records and artifacts of
known age enable us to cross date hundreds of sites in Europe and the Americas within the recent millennia of prehistory. Hence, we have developed the first provisional chronology for a truly global world history and prehistory.

4

SPACE

> After an artifact has been exposed, its position
> must be recorded. This information is as significant
> as the artifact itself.
>
> ROBERT HEIZER, 1958

Space is another vital dimension of archaeological context, not the limitless space of the heavens, but a precisely defined location for every find made during an archaeological survey and excavation. Every archaeological find has an exact location in terms of latitude, longitude, and depth measurement, which together identify any point in space absolutely uniquely. This unique position is measured accurately by systems that we discuss in Chapter 6.

Spatial location is important to archaeologists because it enables them to establish the distances between different objects or dwellings, or between entire settlements, or between settlements and key vegetational zones and landmarks. Such distances may be a few inches of level ground between a fine clay pot and the skeleton of its dead owner or ten miles separating two seasonal camps. A team of fieldworkers may record the distance measurements between dozens of villages that traded luxury goods like seashells over hundreds of miles. We can distinguish two spatial considerations at this point: the distribution of *artifacts within* a settlement, and the distribution of the *settlements themselves*. We return to this latter topic — settlement archaeology — in Chapter 9.

Context in space is closely tied to peoples' behavior. Archaeologists examine both an artifact itself and its association with other artifacts to gain insight into human behavior. The patterning of artifacts around an abandoned iron-smelting furnace or near the bones of a slaughtered bison is good evidence for specific human behavior. An isolated projectile head can tell you only that it was used as a weapon; but the patterning of projectile heads, scraping tools, and large boulders associated with a bison skeleton supplies a context in space that allows much more detailed inferences.

Collections of similar artifacts at contemporary sites within a reasonable geographic range are likely to have been closely related. Such consistent patternings of artifact collections are the basis for classifying "archaeological cultures" and for studying how prehistoric cultures differ over space and through time (Chapter 7).

Space involves archaeologists in two directions of inquiry. The first is part of the process of describing one's finds, of determining the cultural origins of artifacts. This process of ordering is described more fully in Chapter 7, where we discuss some of the arbitrary analytical devices that archaeologists use. The second dimension of space involves studying specific activities — economic, religious, social, technological — within a human settlement. Here again, archaeologists make use of arbitrary analytical units, though ones that are defined by the patterning of artifacts in the ground. These patternings may reflect the activities of a single person, a household, or an entire community.

THE LAW OF ASSOCIATION

In the first analysis, context in space is based on **associations** between artifacts and other evidence of human behavior around them. Let us say you find a beer can opener in a plowed field. An expert on such artifacts — and they do actually exist — can normally date your opener to within a few years of its manufacture by using manufacturers' files or U.S. Patent records. But your beer can opener was an isolated find. No other signs of human activity were discovered nearby. How could you infer, if you were not a twentieth-

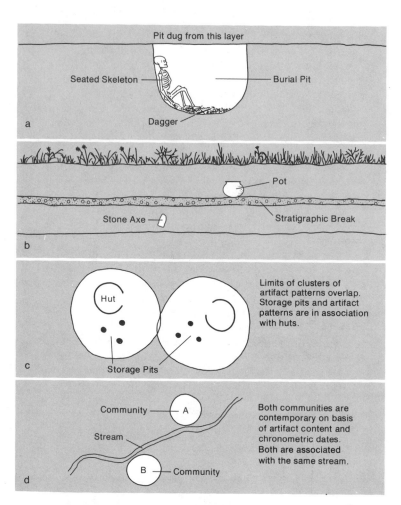

FIGURE 4.1 The law of association: (a) a skeleton associated with a single dagger; (b) a pot and a stone axe, separated by a stratigraphic break, which are not in association; (c) two contemporary household clusters associated with one another; (d) an association of communities that are contemporary.

century American, that the artifact was used for opening a can? But had you found the can opener in association with a dozen punctured beer cans of similar age, you could then infer the general activity that took place, and you could draw some conclusions about the purposes for which the artifact in question was designed.

The law of association is based on the principle that an artifact is contemporary with the other objects found in the precise archaeological horizon in which it is found (Figure 4.1). The proof that humanity was far older than the six thousand years of Biblical chronology came when scientists found ancient stone axes in association with the bones of apparently older extinct animals. The mummy of Egyptian Pharaoh Tutankhamun was associated with an astonishing treasury of household possessions and ritual objects. This association provided unique information on Egyptian life in 1342 B.C.: the mummy alone would have been far less informative.

The law of association is of great importance when one is ordering artifacts in chronological sequences. Many prehistoric societies buried their dead with grave furniture — clay pots, bronze ornaments, seashells, or stone axes. In every case, the objects buried with a corpse were obviously in use when their owner died. Together they are an association of artifacts, a grave group that may be found duplicated in dozens of other contemporary graves. But later graves are found to contain quite different furniture, vessels of a slightly altered form. Obviously, some cultural changes had taken place. When dozens of burial groups are analyzed in this way, the associations and changing artifact styles may provide a basis for dividing the burials into different chronological groups (Figure 4.2).

SUBASSEMBLAGES AND ASSEMBLAGES

Human behavior can be individual and totally unique, shared with other members of one's family or clan, or common to all members of a community. All of these various levels of cultural behavior should, theoretically, be reflected in artifact patterns and associations in the archaeological record. The iron projectile point found in the backbone of a prehistoric war casualty is clearly the consequence of one

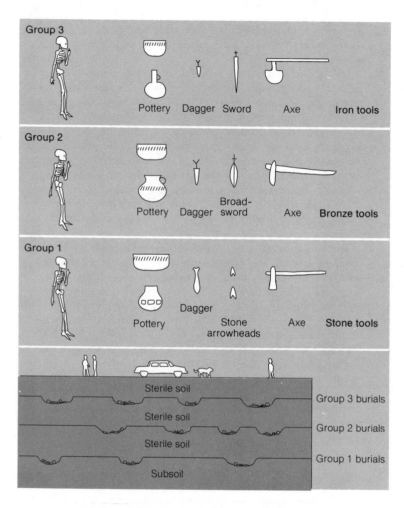

FIGURE 4.2 Burial groups divided into different chronological groups by use of associated artifacts. Group 1 burials contain no metal artifacts, but simply decorated shallow bowls that were made by all burial groups and show cultural continuity through time. The stone arrowheads of Group 1 are replaced by metal swords; daggers continue in use, made successively in stone, bronze, and iron. There is sufficient continuity of artifacts to place groups in sequence, using the law of association; this grouping was in fact confirmed by stratigraphic observation, shown at the bottom.

person's behavior, but that behavior is clearly related to the common cultural behavior of the warrior's society (Figure 4.3).

When more than one artifact is found in a patterned association that reflects the shared cultural behavior of a group of individuals, the artifacts are grouped in **subassemblages**, part of a toolkit that reflects a specific activity. A hunter, for example, uses a bow and arrows, which are carried in a quiver. An auto mechanic uses wrenches, screwdrivers, and gauges. Such subassemblages of artifacts are confined to particular individuals in society.

But what happens when quite dissimilar subassemblages of artifacts — let us say, hunting weapons and baskets and

FIGURE 4.3 An iron arrowhead embedded in the backbone of a prehistoric warrior killed during a battle with Roman soldiers at Maiden Castle, England, in A.D. 43. "The iron arrowhead is clearly the consequence of a single person's behavior, although collectively the warrior's society was engaged in common cultural behavior."

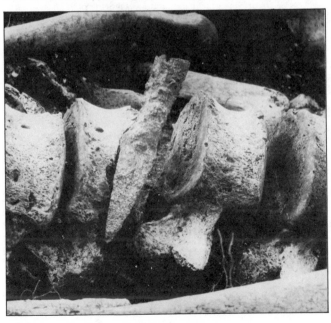

also digging sticks used in collecting plant foods — are found in a contemporary association? The artifacts together reflect in their patterning the shared activities of a total community and are known as an **assemblage**.

This shared behavior is reflected in the remains of houses — in the nonportable artifacts such as storage pits and hearths, inside and outside them — and in community settlement patterns. For example, some early prehistoric Mexican villages consisted of groupings of square, thatched houses. Each house contained subassemblages that reflected the behavior of individual males and females, subassemblages inferred from artifact associations and patternings. The patterned household groups in the village — that is, the associations of these subassemblages and the features associated with them — make up the larger assemblage of human behavior in space that constitutes the entire community (Figure 4.4).

HOUSEHOLDS, COMMUNITIES, AND ACTIVITY AREAS

Archaeological sites are classified by the types of human activity that took place in them. These activities are distinguished through patterning of artifacts and food remains within households and within the settlement. A kill site, for example, is identified from the presence of dismembered bison skeletons associated with scattered stone projectile heads and butchering tools. There are no houses, workshop areas, burials, or storage pits at a kill site; this is simply where the people cut up their prey.

At a two-million-year-old human campsite at Olduvai Gorge, we see a pattern of stone tools, broken bones, boulders, and seeds. In this case, it is hard to infer more than only generalized information from the artifact scatter. It may be possible, for example, to say that the northeast segment of the site was where stone choppers were resharpened, or that bones of larger animals are found only on the outer perimeter of the settlement. But the artifact patterning are so generalized that one can rarely examine the activities of a single household, let alone an individual.

Many later settlements contain the remains of individual houses, each occupied by a group of people who were members of a **household**. In these instances, we can examine the artifacts, hearths, and broken bones within, and around, the confines of a single dwelling, and then compare the activities of individual households. Each house had its own storage areas, garbage pits, and so on, much in the same way that every suburban household has its own garage and garbage cans today (Figure 4.4). All the households in a single settlement make up a **community**.

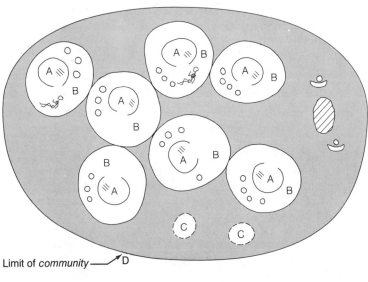

Limit of *community* ⟶ D

O Storage and garbage pits

〰 Hearths

◡ Grinding stones and associated pestles, both subassemblages

▨ Threshing floor

◌ Cattle enclosure

FIGURE 4.4 A hypothetical prehistoric farming village showing: (a) houses; (b) household areas; (c) activity areas; (d) the community; (e) subassemblages. (An assemblage is all of the artifacts from the site.)

Activity areas are identified from characteristic artifact patternings preserved in the ground that reflect a set of tasks, carried out by one or more members of a community (Figure 4.4). Activity areas can normally be identified by mapping a scatter of tools characteristic of a specialist activity such as bead making or stone tool manufacture. Such activities normally took place within a limited area. Under favorable archaeological conditions, these artifact distributions can be used to compare differences in activities between separate households within a community. Some families, for example, may have been specialists in stone knife making, while others made shell beads or were expert metalworkers. The activity areas in these households may reflect such skills.

The behavior of an entire community is reflected in the distribution of houses and households, activity areas, and individual artifacts.

CULTURE AREAS AND SETTLEMENT PATTERNS

But what happens when one considers several communities which share common activities? Activities like big-game hunting, long-distance trade, major religious ceremonies, and so on are often shared by entire cultures and societies. But these behavior patterns can be identified only by patterning of a number of different assemblages at different sites. Such consistent patternings of assemblages represent an **archaeological culture,** the archaeological equivalent of a human society (Chapters 2 and 7). Archaeological cultures consist of material remains of human culture preserved at a specific space and time at several sites. A **culture area** is the geographic area over which the assemblages that make up a unique culture are defined in time and space. An example, from New Zealand, might be the Maori culture area, the region over which the characteristic toolkits of these remarkable peoples are found.

To see how behavior in a prehistoric society as a whole was patterned requires analyzing the ways in which communities and their associated assemblages are distributed on the landscape. Such distributions form **settlement patterns,** which we study with the aid of distribution maps. Many factors interact to determine settlement patterns. These include the natural environment with its seasonal changes, the distribution of plant and animal food resources, peoples' economic practices, and technological skills. Learned cultural patterns and established relationships between different peoples have a compelling influence on settlement patterns in some societies.

The !Kung San hunter-gatherers of the Kalahari Desert live in small camps of a few families by small water holes (Figure 4.5). They move campsites through the year as water supplies become more plentiful or scarcer and vegetable foods within walking distance of each home base are exhausted. Each group of families has a regular set of localities they camp at each year. The amount of time they spend at each varies. The resources of their hunting and gathering territory can support

FIGURE 4.5 A San nuclear family group; a few families live together in campsites near water holes, moving as water supplies increase or diminish.

only a small number of people per square mile, so the different camps are widely dispersed over the landscape. Since the San have no large containers for carrying water or great quantities of food, they return home most nights, having ventured out only as far as they can walk, forage comfortably, and return in daylight. Thus, the !Kung settlement pattern of widely dispersed campsites by water holes results from many interlinked variables.

A settlement pattern and a culture area do not necessarily coincide with one another. The settlement patterns of the Maya in Mesoamerica consisted of large ceremonial centers with elaborate pyramids, temples, plazas, and houses, surrounded by, and linked with, secondary ceremonial centers which in turn were related to a whole hierarchy of lesser settlements. But this Maya settlement pattern is merely one part of the entire Maya cultural system and culture area, the larger area through which characteristic Maya artifact assemblages can be recognized in time and space.

The concepts of culture, time, and space in archaeology are absolutely inseparable. A minimal definition of archaeology is the study of the interrelations between the form of artifacts found in a site, and their date and spatial location. All scientific archaeology, whether survey, excavation, laboratory analysis, or sophisticated theoretical argument encompassing thousands of artifacts, is based on the three critical concepts — form, time, and space — which make up archaeological context.

5

PRESERVATION
AND SURVEY

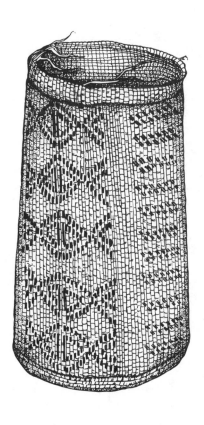

> Antiquities are history defaced, or some remnants
> of history which have casually escaped the ship-
> wreck of time.

FRANCIS BACON, 1605

PRESERVATION

Archaeologists are thought to live in a suspenseful world of rich burials and magnificent treasure houses crammed with gold and dazzling jewels. Object by object, the catalog unfolds as our heroes uncover wonder after new wonder. With breathless suspense, they lift the gilded sarcophagus from the pharaoh's coffin and peer into its mysterious interior. The long-dead king's bandaged corpse stares up at the excited archaeologists. Then, as they watch, the mummy "crumbles to dust on exposure to the outside air." The past has returned to its mysterious oblivion and the archaeologists see fame and fortune slip from their tantalized grasp. Such, we are told, are the fortunes of archaeology.

It is an uncomfortable fact of life that many archaeological finds do crumble to dust once they are exposed to the atmosphere or removed from the environment that has protected them intact for thousands of years. The preservation of delicate finds like mummies, textiles, wooden tools, and the like is a highly technical and time-consuming business. It is a tragedy that so many spectacular archaeological finds were made, in Egypt, the American West, and elsewhere, before the technology of preservation was even partially developed.

The preservation of fragile, organic archaeological remains

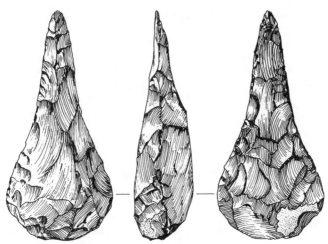

FIGURE 5.1 Acheulian stone axes from Swanscombe on the River Thames, England. "Much of the surviving archaeological record consists of such durable materials in the form of human tools."

like bone, leather, skin, textiles, and wood is dependent on their physical environment. Soil and climatic conditions exercise a very strong influence on archaeological materials. The inorganic artifacts — stone, baked clay pots, mud bricks, gold, copper, and bronze — are those that preserve best. Much of the surviving archaeological record consists of such durable materials in the form of human tools (Figure 5.1).

Prehistoric peoples used many organic substances, materials that survive only at relatively few locations. Bone and antler were commonly used by early hunter-gatherers, especially in Europe some fifteen thousand years ago. The desert peoples of western North America relied heavily on plant fibers and baskets for their material culture. Both hard and soft woods were used for digging-sticks, bows and arrows, and other tools and weapons. Cotton textiles were much prized in coastal Peru two thousand years ago. Nearly every human society collected wild vegetable foods for part of their livelihood. These and traces of broken animal bones and other food remains are sometimes found under favorable preservation conditions.

What are the most favorable preservation conditions for archaeological finds? The fantastically rich tomb of the Egyptian pharoah Tutankhamun, who died in 1342 B.C., yielded incredible finds, including the pharoah's personal wooden furniture, much of his clothing, and the perishable ritual objects that accompanied the dead king to the next world (see Figure 2.2). Tutankhamun's tomb is the only pharaoh's burial ever to be discovered intact and undisturbed by tomb robbers. The richness of the grave furniture came as a complete surprise. And the survival of the funeral bouquets, which showed that the king had died in the spring, was certainly exceptional. Dry conditions like those of the Nile Valley have led to remarkable discoveries in the desert western United States as well, where caves in Utah and Nevada have yielded not only sandals, bows and arrows, and other wood and fiber objects, but thousands of seeds, and even human droppings (coprolites or feces), that can be analyzed to give information on prehistoric diet (Chapter 8).

Waterlogged, flooded sites, too, aid preservation. They can seal off organic finds in an oxygen-free atmosphere. Danish archaeologists have found prehistoric dug-out canoes deep in ancient peat bogs, along with leather clothing, traps, and wooden spears. Their most famous finds are the corpses of sacrificial victims buried in the bogs over two thousand years ago. We can gaze on the serene countenance of Tollund man. His corpse is in such perfect condition that we know he did not eat for at least twenty-four hours before his death, and that his last meal was a porridge of barley and wild grasses (Figure 5.2).

Richard Daugherty has gained unusual insights into prehistoric whale hunting on the northwest coast of America by digging a Makah Indian village at Ozette, Washington, long buried by a series of sudden mudslides. The wet mud crushed a series of cedar plank houses by the ocean, sealing their contents from the destructive effects of the atmosphere. The Ozette village was occupied for over two thousand years, right into the twentieth century. Daugherty's buried houses provided a wealth of information about Makah Indian life and artistic traditions of centuries ago. The thick mud preserved walls and beams, sleeping benches, and fine

FIGURE 5.2 Tollund man, a remarkably well-preserved corpse discovered in the peat bogs of Denmark. "Sites with exceptional preservation conditions are obviously of paramount importance."

mats. Wooden fish hooks, seal-oil bowls, cedar storage boxes, and whaling harpoons were uncovered by using fine water jets from pressure hoses to remove mud from soft wood. The most remarkable find of all was a wooden whale fin carved of red cedar and inlaid with sea otter teeth, a unique ritual object without parallel in North America (Figure 5.3). Fortunate is the archaeologist who finds a site with conditions as perfect as those at Ozette. They are very much the exception rather than the rule.

Arctic cold has virtually frozen the past. When Russian archaeologist Sergei Rudenko excavated the burial mounds of Pazyryk in Siberia, he found long-dead prehistoric horsemen, accompanied by their horses and carts. The sites had literally been refrigerated, so Rudenko recovered not only organic materials, but such fragile objects as Persian rugs, leather horse trappings, even the tattooed skin of the horsemen.

Eskimo archaeology has benefited greatly from frozen soils, for beautiful ivory and bone artifacts have survived almost intact for thousands of years. The Arctic artistic traditions of the north have been dated, by means of changing motifs and styles of harpoons, back thousands of years before the present (Figure 5.4).

But most archaeological sites yield only a fraction of the organic materials which had been buried in them. The fortunate archaeologist may recover not only manufactured tools but some food remains as well — animal bones or a handful of shells, seeds, or other vegetable remains. Obviously the picture one obtains of the inhabitants at such a site is incomplete compared with that from Ozette, Pazyryk, and elsewhere. And, with archaeologists' constant preoccupation with ancient environments and prehistoric lifeways, sites with exceptional preservation conditions are obviously of paramount importance.

FINDING ARCHAEOLOGICAL SITES

How do you know where to dig? How do you find sites or conduct an archaeological survey? Many people are amazed at how archaeologists seem to have an uncanny ability to choose the place for their excavations. Yet, in most cases, they have merely used common sense or well-tried survey techniques to locate their site.

The finding of archaeological sites involves far more than merely locating a prehistoric settlement to dig. Some archaeological sites are so conspicuous that people have always known of their existence. The pyramids of Gizeh in Egypt have withstood the onslaught of tourists, treasure hunters, and quarrymen for thousands of years. The Pyramid of the Sun at Teotihuacán, Mexico, is another easily visible archaeological site (see Figure 9.1). The eastern United States is dotted with hundreds of burial mounds and earthworks, which are easily distinguished from the surrounding coun-

FIGURE 5.3 Richard Daugherty examines a whale fin carved of cedar wood, found at the Ozette site, and inlaid with over 700 sea otter teeth. The teeth at the base are set in the design of a mythical bird with a whale in its talons.

FIGURE 5.4   A walrus ivory object of unknown use of the Ipiutak
culture, *ca.* 1,500 years old, 26 centimeters long. The Arctic artistic
traditions of North America have been dated by means of changing
motifs and styles on bones and ivory artifacts.

tryside. Sites of this type are obviously simple to identify,
and have been known for centuries.

Most archaeological sites are far less conspicuous. They
may consist of little more than a scatter of pottery fragments
or a few stone tools lying on the surface of the ground. Other
settlements may be buried under several feet of soil, leaving
few surface traces except when exposed by water action,
wind erosion, or burrowing animals. Cemeteries may be
marked by piles of stones, while the deep accumulations of
occupation deposits at the mouths of rock shelters or caves or
the huge piles of abandoned shells left by shellfish collectors
are more readily located. The finding of archaeological sites
depends on locating such tell-tale traces of human settlement. Once the sites have been found, they have to be recorded, and surface collections must be made at each locality
to obtain a general impression of the activities of the people
who lived there.

DELIBERATE ARCHAEOLOGICAL SURVEY

An **archaeological survey** can vary from a search of a single
city lot during an afternoon, for traces of historical struc-

tures, to a large-scale survey of an entire river basin or drainage area, over several years. In all cases, the theoretical ideal is easily stated: to record all traces of ancient settlement in the area. But this ideal is impossible to achieve. Many sites leave no traces above the ground. And no survey, however thorough, and however sophisticated its remote sensing devices, will ever achieve the impossible dream of total coverage. The key to effective archaeological survey actually lies in careful design of the research before one sets out in the field, and in the use of techniques to estimate the probable density of archaeological sites in the region.

Archaeological surveys are most effective in terrain where the vegetation is burnt off or sparse enough for the archaeologists to be able to see the ground. In lush vegetation areas like that of the American South, only the most conspicuous earthworks will show up. And, of course, thousands of sites are buried under housing developments, parking lots, and artificial lakes that have radically altered the landscape in many places.

A great deal depends on the intensity of the survey in the field. The most effective surveys are carried out on foot, when the archaeologist can locate the tell-tale traces of artifacts, the grey organic soil eroding from a long-abandoned settlement, and the subtle colors of rich vegetation that reveal the presence of long-buried houses. Plowed fields may display revealing traces of ash, artifacts, or hut foundations. Scatters of broken bones, stone implements, potsherds, or other traces of prehistoric occupation are easily located in such furrowed soil. Observation is the key to finding archaeological sites and to studying the subtle relationships between prehistoric settlements and the landscape on which they flourished.

Archaeologists have numerous inconspicuous signs to guide them. Grey soil from a rodent burrow, a handful of humanly fractured stones in the walls of a desert arroyo, a blurred mark in a plowed field, a potsherd — these are the signs they seek. And oftentime, information on possible sites is provided by knowledgeable local inhabitants.

There is far more to archaeological survey than merely walking the countryside, however. Such surveys can be of varying intensity. The least intensive survey is the most commonplace, one where the investigator examines only conspicuous and accessible sites, those of great size and considerable fame. Heinrich Schliemann did just this when he discovered the site of ancient Troy at Hissarlik in Turkey in the 1870s. John Lloyd Stephens and Frederick Catherwood did the same thing when they visited Uxmal, Palenque, and other Maya sites in Mesoamerica in the early 1840s. Such superficial surveys barely scratch the archaeological surface.

A more intensive survey involves collecting as much information about as many sites as possible from local informants and landowners. Again, the sites located by this means are the larger and more conspicuous ones, and the survey is necessarily incomplete. But this approach is widely used throughout the world, especially in areas where archaeologists have never worked before.

Many more discoveries will be made if the archaeologists undertake a highly systematic survey of a relatively limited area. This type of survey involves not only comprehensive inquiries of local landowners, but actual systematic checking of the site reports on the ground. The footwork resulting from the checking of local reports may lead to more discoveries. But, again, the picture may be very incomplete, for the survey deals with known sites and does not cover the area systematically from one end to the other or establish the proportions of each type of site known to exist in the region.

The most intensive surveys of all have a party of archaeologists covering a whole area by walking all over it, often in straight lines with a set distance between the field workers. When Paul Martin and Fred Plog surveyed 5.2 square miles of the Hay Hollow valley in east-central Arizona in 1967, for example, they supervised a team of eight people who walked back and forth over the area at thirty-foot intervals on carefully established compass lines. They found two hundred and fifty sites in this manner. One would think that with such thoroughness every site would have been discovered, but two entirely new sites came to light in the area several years later!

Clearly, most archaeological surveys can record only a sample of the sites in the survey area, even if the declared objective is to plot the position of every prehistoric settlement. Such has been the purpose of an ambitious survey of the

Basin of Mexico, home of the Teotihuacán and Aztec civilizations of the past two thousand years. The investigators have managed to chronicle the changing settlement patterns in the Basin since long before Teotihuacán rose to prominence after A.D. 100 right up to the Spanish conquest and beyond. But they would be the first to admit that they have only recovered a fraction of the Basin's sites. For a start, most of the Aztec capital, Tenochtitlán, and its outlying suburbs lie under the foundations of Mexico City.

In the past, archaeologists used to look for individual sites. Now, with so many sites being endangered by various types of industrial development, they make an inventory of an archaeological resource base in a specific area. When an area is to be deep-plowed or covered with houses, the burden of proof that archaeological sites do or do not exist in the endangered zone is the responsibility of the archaeologists. Often, time is short and funds are very limited. The only way the archaeologists can estimate the extent of the site resource base is to survey selected areas in great detail. Those areas are determined by use of careful research design and knowledge of the variables that affect site location. The density and distribution of sites in these areas are then used as a basis for generalizing from the sample survey areas to larger regions. The reliability of these vital generalizations is tested through routine statistical procedures.

This approach to archaeological survey is still in its infancy, but will assume great importance as a weapon to counter the wholesale destruction of archaeological sites by industrial activity. There is no way that archaeologists can stop the destruction of every threatened site. The best they can hope for is a chance to make decisions on which sites in the archaeological resource base are to be preserved, which excavated before destruction, and which are to be destroyed in the name of progress. All archaeologists have a responsibility to manage the priceless resource base of sites that is their legacy from the past. This is called **conservation archaeology** or **cultural resource management.**

Obviously, accurate maps and record keeping are essential to any archaeological survey. And there is no point in locating sites without making some attempt to establish their probable content and age. No one has the resources to excavate every site located in a survey, but, in areas where nothing is known, a representative surface collection from all located sites is essential. The artifacts on the surface of a site can give an idea of the occupations and activities that took place there. Surface collections can give little more than a general impression of site contents, for the effects of pot hunting, erosion and weathering, and burrowing animals can decimate surface scatters of artifacts. The site may have been occupied more than once, or may have been the location of some specialist activities such as hunting or stone toolmaking. In cases such as these, every object on a site's surface must be collected according to a carefully formulated sampling design. But even then, surface collection is no real substitute for excavation.

AERIAL PHOTOGRAPHY

The building of today's inventories of archaeological sites would never have been possible without the use of aerial survey techniques. Aerial photography gives an overhead view of the past. Sites can be photographed from many directions, at different times of day, and at various seasons. Numerous sites which have left almost no surface traces on the ground have been discovered by the analysis of air photographs. Many earthworks or other complex structures have been leveled by plows or erosion, but their original layout shows up clearly from the air (Figure 5.5). The rising or setting sun can set off large shadows which emphasize the relief of almost-vanished banks or ditches so that the features of the site stand out in oblique light. Such phenomena are sometimes called "shadow sites."

In some areas, it is possible to detect differences in soil color and in the richness of crop growth on a particular soil. Such marks are hard to detect on the surface but often show up clearly from the air. The growth and color of a crop are greatly determined by the amount of moisture the plant can derive from the soil and subsoil. If the soil depth has been increased by the presence of digging features such as pits and ditches, later filled in, or because additional earth has been heaped up to form artificial banks or mounds, the crops

FIGURE 5.5 A long lost archaeological site revealed by dark crop marks.

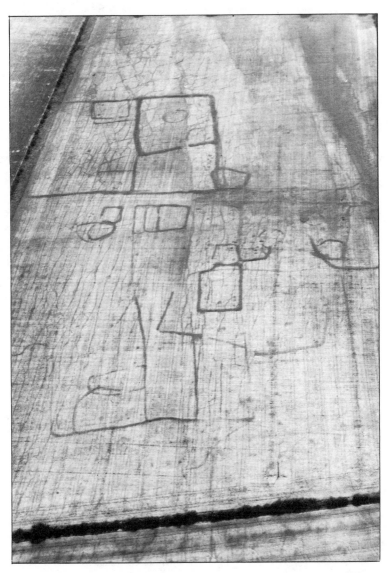

growing over such abandoned structures are high and well nourished. The opposite is also true, in areas where soil has been removed and the infertile soil is near the surface, or where there are impenetrable surfaces such as paved streets below ground level and the crops grow less thickly. Thus, a dark crop mark can be taken for a ditch or pit, while a lighter line will define a more substantial structure.

Much of the world has been photographed from twenty-four thousand feet by military photographers. Such coverage has been put to use by archaeologists to survey remote areas such as the Virú Valley in Peru, where a team of archaeologists led by Gordon Willey plotted 315 sites on a master map of the valley. Many of the sites were stone buildings or agricultural terraces, others were refuse mounds that appeared as low hillocks on the photographs. By using aerial surveys, Willey saved days of survey time, for he was able to pinpoint many sites before going out in the field. When the settlements were visited, a fascinating story of shifting settlement patterns in Virú over thousands of years emerged from a combination of foot survey and air photography.

REMOTE SENSING

Aerial remote-sensing devices of many types have been developed in recent years to complement the valuable results obtained from black and white photography. Infrared film, which has three layers sensitized to green, red, and infrared, detects reflected solar radiation at the near end of the electromagnetic spectrum, some of which is invisible to the naked eye. The different reflections from various cultural and natural features are translated by the film into distinctive "false" colors. Vigorous grass growth on river plains shows up bright red. Such red patterns have been used in the American Southwest to track shallow, subsurface water sources where there were formerly springs used by prehistoric peoples. The infrared data could lead the archaeologist to likely areas for previously undetected hunting camps and villages.

In some areas, exuberant vegetation hampers archaeological surveys, especially in the Maya lowlands. For years, archaeologists have wondered how the Maya civilization managed to feed itself and have puzzled over the incompletely known distribution of its cities and ceremonial centers. Originally they believed that the Maya population was supported by "slash and burn" cultivation, a system still used today, in which people burn off and clear the forests, then cultivate the land for three or four years before leaving it fallow and moving on to new virgin plots. But so many sites are now known that we can be certain that the population was far larger than such a simple agricultural system could handle. Some surveys and excavations suggested that the Maya may have drained swamps and used irrigated lands, but no large-scale fieldwork was possible in the hot and densely overgrown rain forest.

A group of archaeologists, looking for a sensor system that would penetrate the dense forest cover of the area and see through silt and root cover to map ancient roads, causeways, and other humanly made structures invisible on the surface, discovered an unexpected archaeological payoff in the imaging radar developed by NASA for spaceborne lunar sounders and synthetic aperture radar. (The particular radar chosen for the Maya experiment was, in fact, developed for imaging the surface of the planet Venus.) A series of flights were made over the Maya lowlands in 1978 and 1980, using black and white and color infrared film to search for indications of archaeological sites and ancient landscape modifications. When the features discovered were plotted onto topographic maps, they revealed not only shadows from large mounds and buildings, but irregular grids of gray lines within swampy areas near known major sites. These lines were found to form ladder-and-lattice as well as curvilinear patterns, which matched conventional aerial views of known canal systems from the Valley of Mexico and the lowlands very closely. The investigators believe that further radar surveys will reveal that the Maya grew large food surplusses using large-scale swamp agriculture, developing field systems that are virtually invisible on the ground today, but the method is still experimental.

The trouble with space-age devices like radar sensors is that their cost is out of reach for most archaeological budgets, but fortunately, there are some geophysical prospecting tools that are of more moderate cost. They are of great use when a site has already been located and the archaeologist wants to find buried subsurface features such as stone walls. A restivity survey meter, for instance, is sometimes used to measure the variations in the resistance (restivity) of the ground to electric current. Stone walls or hard pavement retain less dampness than a deep pit filled with soft earth or a silted-up ditch. These differences can be measured accurately with a restivity meter, which records the restivity "contours" across a grid of squares laid out on the site. On well-drained soils, restivity surveys can locate the drier areas where buried ditches and walls lie.

Most people are familiar with the mine detector, a device used by many beachcombers and treasure hunters to search for loot. Although the companies selling such devices often promote them as a means of finding wealth in the ground, archaeologists have turned such electromagnetic detection devices to good use to find iron objects, fired clay furnaces, hearths, and pottery kilns. A proton magnetometer is used to measure the differences between the remnant magnetism of undisturbed soil and that of nearby subsurface features like pottery kilns that have been heated in the past. The heated features retain a weak magnetism different from that of the earth's magnetic field. Magnetic detecting has been used very successfully to record pits, walls, and other features in the middle of large fortified towns and in ceremonial centers where total excavation of a site is clearly uneconomic.

ACCIDENTAL DISCOVERIES

Whole chapters of the past have emerged through accidental discoveries of sites, spectacular artifacts, or skeletons. Dramatic finds have resulted from despoiling of the environment. Deep plowing and freeway and dam construction have led to the uncovering — and damaging — of priceless sites. When Mexico City's Metro was tunneled under the modern city, the twenty-eight miles of tunnels yielded a wealth of archaeological material. Mexico City is built on the site of the Aztec city of Tenochtitlán, overthrown by Hernando Cortés in 1521. Little remains of the Aztec city on the surface today. But the contractors for the Metro recovered forty tons of pottery, 380 burials, and even a small temple dedicated to the wind god Ehecatl-Quetzalcoatl. The temple is now preserved on its original site as part of the Piño Suarez station of the Metro system. All the tunneling operations were under the supervision of expert archaeologists, who were empowered to halt construction whenever an archaeological find was made.

The fields of the Western world have yielded many caches of buried weapons, coins, smith's tools, and sacrificial objects, valued treasures that were buried in times of stress by their owners. For whatever reason, the owners never returned to recover their valuables. Thousands of years later, a farmer comes across the hoard and, if a responsible citizen, reports the find to archaeological authorities. If not, yet another valuable fragment of the past is lost to science.

Nature itself sometimes uncovers sites for us, which are then located by a sharp-eyed archaeologist looking for natural exposures of likely geological strata. Olduvai Gorge is a great gash in the Serengeti Plains of northern Tanzania. An ancient earthquake opened a deep gorge, exposing hundreds of feet of lake bed that had been buried long before. It is these buried lake deposits that have yielded early campsites dating to at least 1.75 million years ago. They would never have been found without the assistance of an earthquake and subsequent erosion. The Olduvai area is but one of many examples from all over the world where nature has revealed the incredible bounty of the past.

The archaeologist of today is concerned not only with the discovery of sites but with their preservation and management as well. The archaeological record consists of thousands of sites that can never be replaced. In a sense, all archaeologists are managers of this archive. More and more archaeological surveys are conducted in advance of bulldozers and major construction projects. Often archaeologists have to estimate how many sites in an area remain undiscovered after their survey, and then recommend to federal or state agencies what measures, if any, should be taken to minimize the impact of a major land-use project on the archaeological resources they have discovered. This type of archaeological survey is still in its infancy. It results from recent local, state, and federal legislation that recognizes that archaeological sites are an important natural resource. And the stakes are high. Without adequate surveys and resource management efforts, it is safe to say that the future of archaeology in some parts of the world, especially North America and western Europe, would be in grave doubt. There would simply be nothing left for science.

6

EXCAVATION

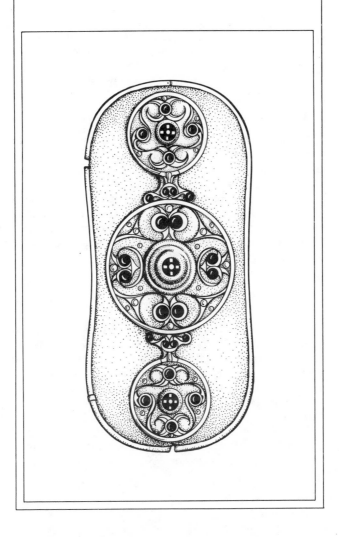

A mere hole in the ground, which of all sights is perhaps the least vivid and dramatic, is enough to grip their attention for hours at a time.

P. G. WODEHOUSE, 1919

Modern archaeological excavation is a precise and demanding science, which has the objective of recording archaeological sites and their contents in exact detail. This chapter describes some of the basic principles of excavation and some of the many excavation problems that archaeologists can encounter in the field. It should be emphasized, however, that each site presents distinctive problems and requires modification of the basic principles enumerated below.

EXCAVATION

The first principle of excavation is that digging is destruction. The archaeological deposits so carefully examined during a dig are destroyed forever in the process. Site contents are removed to a laboratory, permanently divorced from their context in time and space in the ground. Here is a radical difference from other disciplines. A chemist can readily recreate the conditions of a basic experiment. The historian can return to the archives for a reevaluation of the complex events in a politician's life. But an archaeologist's archives are destroyed during the dig. All that remains from an excavation are the finds from the trenches, the unexcavated portions of the site, and the photographs, notes, and drawings that record the excavator's observations for posterity. One of the tragedies of archaeology is that much available archaeological data has been excavated under far from scientific conditions. Our archives of information are uneven at best.

The treasure hunter destroys a site in search of valuable finds, and keeps no records. Archaeologists destroy sites as well, but with a difference. They create archives of archaeological information that document contexts for the objects they take back to the laboratory with them. Although they have destroyed their site forever, they have created a data bank of information in its place, the only archive their successors will be able to consult to check their results. Archaeologists have serious responsibilities: for recording and interpreting the significance of the layers, houses, food remains, and artifacts in their sites, and for publishing the results for posterity. Without accurate records and meaningful publication of results of an excavation, archaeological investigation is useless. Regrettably, far too many interesting and important excavations have never been recorded in print and the results are lost forever.

A generation ago, archaeologists' first inclination was to dig sites to solve problems. Nowadays, there is increased awareness that excavation destroys irreplaceable evidence of the past, and they dig only when they have to. Anyone who digs without experience of record keeping and all the other processes of serious excavation is committing vandalism of an unforgivable kind. No treasure hunting or pot collecting, please!

RESEARCH DESIGN

It follows that any archaeological excavation must be conducted from a sound research design that seeks to solve specific problems. This research design can be a simple one, posing simple questions that need to be tested against data excavated from the ground. How old is that burial mound? Who occupied that village site, when, and what did they live on? What is the sequence of human cultures at Olduvai

Gorge? The research design is created in the first stages of an investigation before a single trench has been dug or the crew assembled. As the dig begins, stratigraphy must be recorded and dates determined. Once basic questions are answered, research objectives may change, becoming very detailed or highly complex.

The end products of even a month's excavation on a moderately productive site are boxes upon boxes of potsherds, stone tools, bones, and other finds that have to be cleaned, sorted, marked, and studied once the excavation is complete. Rolls of drawings completed in the field contain valuable stratigraphical information. So do slides, photographs, and hundreds of pages of field notes compiled by the director of the excavation as the long days of digging continue. Radiocarbon and soil samples are collected for analysis. Freshwater shells and charcoal fragments are packed ready for shipment to specialist investigators. One expert excavator once told me it took a minimum of six months to analyze the finds from a month's excavation. The dozens of boxes and hundreds of notebook pages contain a large array of interconnected facts that have to be joined together to reconstruct the site in its original state. The research design is constantly reevaluated to determine the future course of the dig. The days when a site was dug simply because it "looked good" are long gone.

Illinois archaeologists Stuart Struever and James Brown have spent many field seasons excavating the Koster site in the lower Illinois River Valley. Here, at least twelve human occupations are represented at one site, the earliest of which dates to before 5100 B.C. Koster is a deep site, probably abandoned before A.D. 1000 after generations of Indians had settled at this favorable locality. It offered Brown and Struever a unique opportunity to examine the changing cultures of the inhabitants over a period of more than six thousand years. But the organizational problems were enormous. Koster is over thirty feet deep, with each of the twelve cultural horizons separated from its neighbor by zones of sterile soil. Brown and Struever were fortunate in being able to treat each occupation level of this mammoth site as an entirely separate digging operation.

The archaeologists had two options. One was to dig small

test trenches and obtain samples of pottery and other finds from each stratigraphic level. But this approach, though cheaper and commonly used, was inadequate for the problems to be investigated at the Koster site. The excavators were interested in studying the origins of agriculture in the lower Illinois Valley. So Brown and Struever decided to excavate each living surface on a sufficiently large scale to study the activities that had taken place there. This would enable them to examine minute economic changes. Thus, the emphasis in the Koster excavations was on isolating the different settlement types that lay one on top of the other.

In developing the Koster research design, Brown and Struever needed to control a mass of complex variables that affected their data. They had to develop special procedures to ensure the statistical validity of their excavations. In order to acquire immediate feedback on the finds made during the excavations, they organized an elaborate data-processing system that sorted the animal bones, artifacts, vegetable remains, and other discoveries on location in the field. The tabulated information on each sorted find was then fed by remote access terminal to a computer many miles away. Within a few days, the excavators had instant access to the latest data from the dig. This means that overall research design can be modified while an excavation is still in progress.

The Koster site is a fine example of elaborate research design that uses complex computer technology. The dig employed dozens of people each field season. Most excavations operate on a far smaller scale, but the ultimate principles are the same: sound research design, very careful recording of all data, and scientifically controlled excavation. The Koster excavation was designed, like all good digs, to solve specific research problems formulated in the context of a sound research design.

TYPES OF EXCAVATION

How do you decide where to dig? What tools do you use, and why are your trenches this shape? How deep do you excavate? People always seem to ask these same questions when they visit an excavation. Below we discuss different types of archaeological sites and the problems they create for excavators. Here now are some general principles.

You can decide where to dig on a site by simple, arbitrary choice of a spot which has yielded a large number of surface finds or one where traces of stone walls or other ancient structures can be seen above the ground. When Richard Daugherty dug the Ozette site on the Washington coast, he began by digging through the place where the largest occupation sequence seemed to be. Why? He simply needed to obtain as complete a cultural sequence as he could. The logical way to do so was to dig through the deepest part of the site. There was, of course, no guarantee that his trench would penetrate to the earliest part of the whale hunters' site. But his choice was a logical way to start attacking the fundamental questions of when and for how long the whale hunters lived at Ozette. Similar decisions have been made at thousands of other sites all over the world.

In the days of high digging costs, today's archaeologists rely more heavily on statistical sampling then their predecessors. Sampling is used in digging shell heaps or dense accumulations of occupation debris containing thousands of artifacts. Obviously, only a small sample of a large garbage heap can be dug and analyzed. To assure validity of the statistical samples, some form of sampling technique must be used to choose which part of a site is to be dug in an unbiased way.

Sampling has been defined as the "science of controlling and measuring the reliability of information through the theory of probability." Sampling techniques allow us to ensure a statistically reliable basis of archaeological data from which we can make generalizations about our research data. Most archaeologists make use of **probabilistic sampling,** for the discipline of statistics and statistical theory makes considerable use of probability theory, a means of relating small samples of data in mathematical ways to much larger populations. The classic example of this is the political opinion poll, which samples national feelings on the basis of tiny samples, perhaps as few as 1,500 people. In archaeological terms, probabilistic sampling improves the likelihood that the conclusions reached from a survey or excavation on the basis of the samples are relatively reliable.

The use of formal sampling techniques in archaeology is

still in an initial stage. Simple **random sampling** is quite commonly used, as when an archaeologist wishes to obtain an unbiased sample of artifacts from an ancient shell mound. One can do this by laying out a rectangular grid of squares on a site and then selecting the squares to be dug by using a table of random numbers (Figure 6.1). The excavated samples are thus chosen at random, rather than on the basis of surface finds or other considerations. Archaeological sampling, based as it is on descriptive and inferential statistics, is a complex subject that is still in its infancy. The interested reader is urged to consult the references at the end of this book.

FIGURE 6.1 A hypothetical dig with trenches laid out by using a random sampling table. That is, the trench layout is completely by chance, with the cuttings to be dug selected from a table of randomly selected numbers.

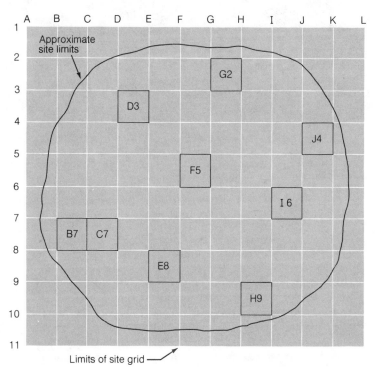

FIGURE 6.2   Vertical excavation in Coxcatlán Cave in Tehuacán Valley,
Mexico. The large pits result from the excavation of alternate squares
as separate units. Coxcatlán had yielded some of the earliest evidence
for maize cultivation in the world.

Vertical Excavation

The layout of small digs is determined not only by surface
features, density of surface finds, or sampling techniques,
but by available funds as well. Most excavations are run on
shoe-string budgets, so small-scale operations have to be
used to solve complex problems with minimum expenditure
of time and money. Some of the world's most important
sites, like, for example, Coxcatlán Cave in the Tehuacán Valley, Mexico (Figure 6.2), have been excavated on a small
scale by vertical excavation, where limited areas are dug for

FIGURE 6.3 Area excavation of an Iroquois long house near Onondaga, New York. The small stakes indicate positions of house wall posts; hearth areas and support posts can be seen inside the walls.

specific information on dating and stratigraphy. Vertical trenches can be used to obtain artifact samples, to establish sequences of ancient building construction or histories of complex earthworks, and to salvage sites threatened by destruction. The small trenches are often dug in areas where the deposits are likely to be of maximum thickness or where important structures are likely to be found.

Area Excavation

Large-scale excavations are normally used to uncover wider areas of a site. These horizontal, or area, excavations are used to uncover house plans and settlement layouts. They are expensive (Figure 6.3). The only sites that are completely excavated are very small hunter-gatherer camps, isolated huts, or burial mounds. With larger settlements, all one can do is uncover a portion of the settled area in the hope that it is representative of the entire settlement.

Area excavations expose large, open areas of ground to a depth of several feet. A complex network of walls or abandoned storage pits may lie within the area to be investigated. Each of these ancient features relates to other structures, a relationship which must be carefully recorded if the site is to be interpreted correctly. If the area excavated is large, this immediately creates a serious recording problem. The excavators use a grid of squares, each with its own letter and number, to aid in digging and recording the site (Figure 6.4a). For excavating the surviving remains of an Indian long house or a scatter of artifacts left by a prehistoric craftsman, accurate recording techniques are obviously essential (Figure 6.4b).

DIGGING, TOOLS, AND PEOPLE

How do you do the digging? Much depends on the type of site you are excavating. A huge burial mound on the Ohio River may be over twenty feet long. Much of the sterile deposit covering the burial levels is removed with picks and shovels. But as soon as the archaeologists reach layers where finds are expected, they dig with meticulous care, removing each layer in turn, recording the exact position of their finds upon discovery. Smaller caves or cemeteries are excavated inch by inch. The earth surrounding the finds is passed through fine screens so that tiny beads, fish bones, and a myriad of other small items can be found.

Excavation is in part a recording process, and accuracy is essential. The records will never be precise unless the dig is kept tidy at all times. The trench walls must always be straight. Why? So you can record the layers you are digging and follow them across the site. Surplus soil is dumped well away from the trenches so it does not cascade into the dig. The excavation is a laboratory and must be treated as such.

All archaeological digs are headed by a director, who is responsible both for organizing the excavation and for overseeing the specialists and diggers under her or his supervision. Many larger digs will involve a team of specialist ex-

FIGURE 6.4 (a) Two trenches laid out with a grid. (b) Three-dimensional recording of the position of an object using the grid squares.

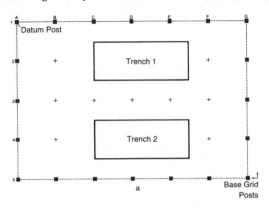

a

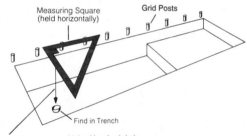

Vertical measurement obtained by plumb-bob and string hung above object.

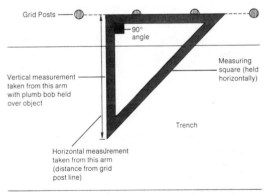

b

perts who work alongside the excavators. At the Ozette site, for example, Richard Daugherty had the cooperation of a geologist and a zoologist who visited the site regularly. They studied the geological background of the settlement and the many animal bones found as the dig proceeded. A really large excavation in Mesopotamia or Mesoamerica can involve dozens of people — specialist archaeologists, a team of resident experts in other fields, graduate student trainees, and volunteer or paid workers who do much of the actual excavation. We describe some of the ways you can obtain digging experience in Chapter 10.

Archaeologists use many digging tools in their work. Picks, shovels, and long-handled spades carry the brunt of the heavy work. But the most common archaeological tool is the diamond-shaped trowel, with its straight edges and sharp tip. With it, soil can be eased from a delicate specimen or an unusual discoloration in the soil scraped clean. Trowels are used for tracing delicate layers in walls, clearing small pits, and other fine jobs. They are rarely out of the digger's hand.

Household and paint brushes often come in handy, the former for cleaning trenches and the latter for freeing fragile objects from the soil. Even fine artists' brushes have their uses for cleaning beads, decaying ironwork, or fine bones in human burials. Enterprising archaeologists visit their dentists regularly, if only to obtain regular supplies of worn-out dental instruments, which make first-rate fine digging tools! So do six-inch nails ground to different shapes. A set of fine screens for sifting soil for small finds, several notebooks and graph paper, tapes, plumb bobs, surveyors' levels, and a compass are just a few of the items that archaeologists need to record their excavations and to process their finds.

RECORDING

No dig is worth more than its records. The excavation notebooks provide a day-by-day record of each trench, of new layers and significant finds. Before a single trench is measured out, the entire site is laid out on a grid of squares. Important finds, or details of a house or a storage pit, are measured in on the site plan by using simple, three-dimensional recording techniques (Figure 6.4b). It is information from your records, as well as the artifacts from the dig, that form the priceless archive of your excavation. If the records are incomplete, the dig is little better than a treasure hunt.

Let us now turn from general principles to some specific excavation problems that will give you an insight into the multitude of challenges awaiting field workers. As we indicated in Chapter 2, archaeological sites, in all shapes and sizes, are the basis of all field investigations. All contain traces of human activity, in the form of artifacts, structures, and food remains. Archaeologists most commonly classify sites by their functions, that is to say, by the activities that took place within them. It is no coincidence that these various site categories present different excavation problems.

HABITATION SITES

Hunter-Gatherer Campsites

Habitation sites are the most common of all archaeological sites, places where people have lived and carried out many different activities. Some of the earliest habitation sites in the world are those at Olduvai Gorge, Tanzania, where Louis and Mary Leakey not only recovered tools, animal bones, and human fossils, but, by careful excavation, were able to record the position of every artifact and bone on the living surface (Figure 6.5). Tons of sterile soil had to be removed before the Leakeys were able to lay out a grid of squares over the floors, which were then dug in strips. The position of every object on the site surface was then plotted before the finds were marked and removed.

The Olduvai campsites were occupied only for a few days or weeks about 1.75 million years ago. On one floor, the Leakeys found more than four thousand artifacts and bones scattered over an area fifteen feet in diameter. Outside the main scatter lay another pile of bones and tools. They speculated that a crude shelter of branches that had vanished without trace separated the main scatter from the outlying bones. By careful excavation with trowel, brush, and dental pick at a slightly earlier site, Mary Leakey uncovered a semicircular stone pavement that may have been a foundation for another shelter — perhaps the earliest known human habitation in the world.

The same careful area excavation techniques are used at other hunter-gatherer campsites. Concentrations of dismembered animal carcasses, sleeping places, hearths, or piles of

FIGURE 6.5 Excavation of a campsite at Olduvai Gorge, Tanzania.

flaked stone debris are all elements in a habitation site that can be related one to another by area excavation.

Caves and Rockshelters

The mouth of a cave or a rocky overhang in a cliff were favorite homes of prehistoric people. Huge accumulations of occupation debris extending over thousands of years are to be found in the great rockshelters and caves of the Dordogne Valley of southwest France, where prehistoric hunter-gatherers flourished from forty thousand to ten thousand years ago and painted exquisite pictures of the animals they hunted. Danger and Hogup Caves in Utah contain thousands of years of hunter-gatherer occupation. The dry environment of the desert has preserved wooden objects and basketry, as well as minute details of economic life. And the dry caves of Tehuacán Valley in northern Mexico have provided a unique history of the development of maize cultivation in the New World (Chapter 8).

Cave and rockshelter excavations are some of the hardest digs to carry through successfully. The ground below the cliff overhangs usually consists of ash and other debris piled up through successive human occupations. Sterile soils may interrupt this sequence of habitation, representing periods when the site was abandoned. Excavating such complicated sequences is slow and meticulous work. The trenches are normally restricted by the size of the shelter. Each hearth and small occupation layer has to be isolated from the others during excavation.

Many cave and rockshelter excavations are concerned purely with dating and stratigraphy, but others are more ambitious. When Hallam Movius dug the Abri Pataud rockshelter in France, he had to record at least six layers of human occupation dated to between forty thousand and nine thousand years ago, extending to over twenty feet of stratified deposit. The site was excavated on a coordinated, master plan basis that involved not only archaeologists but botanists, geologists, and other specialists as well. Movius was able to record minute changes in tool types and to record many details of the changing hunting and gathering practices of Abri Pataud's inhabitants.

Mounds

Occupation mounds (often called "tells" in the Near East) are commonplace in many parts of the world. Mound sites result when the same site is occupied for centuries, even thousands of years. Successive generations lived atop their predecessors' settlements. The result is a gradual accumulation of occupation debris, which, when excavated, provides a complicated picture of occupation levels.

Even a small mound can cost a fortune to excavate, simply because the lowest levels are so deeply buried below the surface. A huge mound like that of Ur-of-the-Chaldees in Mesopotamia, or Tepe Yahya in Iran, can be sampled only by large trenches that cut into the sides of the mound in a series of great steps, or by very large-scale excavation indeed, using a combination of vertical and area trenches (Figure 6.6). There is far more to excavating an occupation mound than merely stripping off successive occupation layers. So many natural and artificial processes, ranging from wind erosion to human activity, can change the stratigraphy of a

FIGURE 6.6   Tepe Yahya, Iran, a typical Near Eastern city mound, or *tell*. The stepped trenches of the excavation can be seen in the slope of the mound.

site of this type that each site presents a challenging new excavation problem.

Earthworks and Forts

Many peoples — Iron Age peasants in western Europe, Maori warriors in New Zealand, Hopewell Indians in Ohio — built extensive earth fortifications to protect their settlements or sacred places. The Ohio earthworks enclose large areas of ground, but no one knows exactly why such earthworks were undertaken. To excavate them would require both vertical excavation to record cross sections across the earthworks, and area investigation to uncover the layout of the structures built inside the earthworks. Such excavations were indeed carried out on the great prehistoric fortress at Maiden Castle, England, many years ago. The massive earthworks of Maiden Castle were stormed by a Roman legion in A.D. 43. By careful excavation and use of historical data, the excavator Mortimer Wheeler was able to write a blow-by-blow description of the battle for the fortress (Figure 6.7).

FIGURE 6.7 The Iron Age hill fort at Maiden Castle, Dorset, England; its extensive earthworks were excavated by Mortimer Wheeler.

Shell Middens

Shell middens, which are vast accumulations of abandoned shells, fish bones, and other food remains, are commonplace in many coastal areas of the world. Remarkable results can be obtained from studying these dense heaps, especially in the reconstruction of prehistoric diets (Chapter 8). The excavation problem is twofold: first, to identify the stratified levels in the middens, and second, to obtain statistically reliable samples of food remains and artifacts from the deposits. Most shell midden digs are laid out by use of random cuttings, described very briefly earlier. We illustrate an example of an area excavation on a New Zealand shell midden (Figure 6.8), where much information on ancient diet was obtained by using a carefully laid out grid of trenches. The excavation of a shell midden is normally a rather unspectacular process, for the detailed statistical results come from laboratory analysis of artifacts rather than from actual digging. Hopefully, one can look at ways in which the inhabitants utilized different communities of shellfish, like oysters of different sizes, through time.

CEREMONIAL AND OTHER SPECIALIST SITES

Some of the world's most famous archaeological sites are ceremonial centers like the pyramids of Gizeh in Egypt or the Maya ceremonial center at Copán, Honduras. Many ceremonial sites are of enormous size, and, like occupation mounds, present great difficulties for the excavator. Teotihuacán in the Valley of Mexico is, of course, far more than a ceremonial center (see Figure 9.1). It was a great city as well, which flourished from 200 B.C. to as late as A.D. 750. To discover the true significance of the site has involved not only extensive area excavation designed to aid in the reconstruction of pyramids and major buildings, but sophisticated mapping and surface survey combined with small-scale excavation as well. René Millon and other archaeologists have mapped over twelve and a half square miles of Teotihuacán, in a survey program combined with some excavation. Their aim is to give a comprehensive picture of the huge city as it rapidly developed into a religious and ceremonial center of wide importance.

FIGURE 6.8 An exemplary area excavation of a shallow shell midden at Galatea Bay, New Zealand. "The detailed statistical results come from laboratory analysis rather than from actual digging."

With trading sites, quarries and other specialized sites, as well as with ceremonial centers, one major concern is with the artifact patternings coming from the excavations. Do these patterns reflect long-distance trading activity in, say, copper ornaments or seashells? Are marine sting-ray spines, which are present in what appear to be temples built hundreds of miles inland, artifacts of great religious significance in Mexico? It is questions like these that can be answered only by careful studies of artifact patterning.

BURIALS AND CEMETERIES

Human burials are the stereotypic finds of archaeology, reflecting humanity's abiding concern with the afterlife. The earliest human burials were left by Neanderthal peoples seventy thousand years ago. Most human societies have paid

FIGURE 6.9 A classic Maya collective tomb at Guattan in the Mota-gua Valley, Guatemala.

careful attention to funerals and burials ever since. Many burials were deposited with simple or elaborate grave furniture, designed to accompany its owner to the afterlife.

People have buried their dead in isolated, shallow graves within their settlement, in special cemeteries, in caves, cremated in jars, and in vast burial mounds. Some burials consist of the skeleton alone, others lie with a few beads or a handful of clay pots (Figure 6.9). Royal personages have been buried in all their glory: Shang kings in China with their chariots; the rulers of early Ur-of-the-Chaldees, Mesopotamia, with their entire court; Maya nobles with their prize treasures.

By studying a group of burials from a single cemetery, it may be possible to distinguish different social classes by the grave furniture buried with the skeleton. The common people may take nothing with them, while merchants or priests may be buried with distinctive artifacts associated with their status in society. The Adena and Hopewell peoples of North America, for example, were much concerned with the afterlife during their heyday two thousand years ago. From the distribution of the burials and cemeteries in their burial mounds, and from the cult objects and ornaments associated with the skeletons, it may be possible to gain some insights into the social organization of Adena and Hopewell societies (Chapter 9). And, of course, burials are a fruitful source of information on personal ornamentation and appearance, too, for people were (and still are) often buried in the clothes and ornaments they wore in life. The physical characteristics of the skeletons themselves can provide valuable data on age, nutrition, sex, and ancient disease.

How does one excavate a burial? Whether one is digging a large cemetery or a single burial, each skeleton and its associated grave, ornaments, and grave goods are considered a single excavation problem. Each burial is dug as a single unit which has both internal associations with its accompanying goods and external associations with other burials in the same and other levels. The first step is to identify the grave, either by locating a gravestone or a pile of stones, or from the grave outlines, which may appear as a discoloration in the surrounding soil. Once the grave outlines have been found, individual bones are exposed. The main outline of the burial is traced first. Then you uncover the fingers, toes, and other small bones. You leave the bones in place and take care not to displace any ornaments or grave furniture associated with them. Once the skeleton is exposed and fully cleaned where it lies, the layout of the burial and grave furniture is recorded by drawings and photographs before the skeleton is lifted bone by bone or encased in a cocoon of plaster of paris and metal strips (Figure 6.9).

Burial excavation may seem very romantic. In reality it is not only technically demanding, but raises important ethical questions as well. For years archaeologists casually dug up Indian burials, many of them only a few generations old. Now Indians are objecting strenuously to excavation and destruction of ancient burial grounds — and with good reason. Why should their ancestors be dug and displayed in museums, they argue. Many surviving communities retain strong emotional and religious ties with their ancestors, links that must be respected by archaeologist, developer, and historian alike. The sensitive excavator will always leave the recent dead undisturbed and reserve burial investigation for sites with no spiritual links to the present.

7

ORDERING
THE PAST

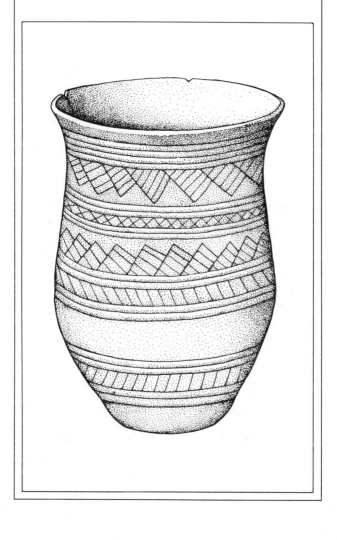

Order is Heav'n's first law

ALEXANDER POPE, *An Essay on Man*

BACK FROM THE FIELD

Archaeologists spend much more time in their laboratories than they do excavating and surveying. They must, for the finds from even a brief excavation can take months to sort, classify, and analyze. The field crew returns from the dig with truckloads of boxes and bags full of unsorted stone tools, pot fragments, broken animal bones, and other finds. There are precious cartons containing human skeletons and rows of radiocarbon and soil samples for specialists to examine. It can take some days simply to organize these piles of boxes in the laboratory before the real work begins. Then, once the tables are clear, the long process of describing and ordering all the finds from the dig starts.

The laboratory crew — normally graduate students and undergraduates working under supervision — begin by sorting all the finds into very broad categories. Soil and radiocarbon samples are sent off to experts. Animal bones, seeds, and other food remains are separated from manufactured artifacts and handed over to the members of the team who are skilled in identifying such finds. The artifacts themselves are sorted into broad classes, pot fragments separated from stone implements, metal tools handled separately from shell beads, and so on. The labeling of every bag and box is carefully checked. Properly marked containers must note the three-dimensional unit of space and time in which the ma-

112

terials were found (see Figure 6.4). Everything is now ready for basic classification and ordering of the manufactured artifacts. This chapter describes some of the ways archaeologists tackle these complex tasks.

CLASSIFICATION AND TAXONOMY

Before joining the archaeologists in their laboratory as they classify and order their finds, we should remember that everyone classifies things in day-to-day life. We distinguish between Chevrolets and Fords, between knives and forks, cups and saucers. Archaeologists use classification as a research tool for ordering and making sense of large quantities of artifacts. The objectives of archaeological classification change from one problem to another, but in every case classification is a means to the solution of a specific archaeological problem.

Every science, be it archaeology, botany, chemistry, or physics, requires a body of basic units of classification, or **taxonomy,** used for categorizing data as a basis for explaining scientific phenomena. Biologists, for instance, classify all living things in a formal taxonomy. *Homo sapiens sapiens,* the modern human being, is a subspecies of the species *Homo sapiens. Homo sapiens* is a member of the genus *Homo.* All are in the family *Hominidae,* and so on. The relationships between these various terms are clearly understood by everyone using them, for this biological taxonomy is in universal use.

There is still no generally accepted archaeological taxonomy used all over the world. British archaeologists, for example, refer to "cultures," North Americans to "phases," and the French to "periods." Each of these terms means roughly the same thing, but there are subtle differences that result from different attitudes to archaeology and contrasting field situations. All this is very confusing, not the least to archaeologists themselves. All archaeologists do agree, at least, that their classifications of artifacts are designed to simplify making comparisons between assemblages from different sites. They also agree that the purpose of taxonomy is to make both chronological and cultural relationships between different sites and areas easier to understand.

Attributes

Let us now look over the shoulder of a group of student archaeologists as they sat down to the analysis of the pottery fragments (potsherds) from their recently excavated site. The director of the laboratory team set his students to work separating and then counting and weighing all the undecorated potsherds. They were then discarded. A much smaller collection of potsherds, all decorated, now lay on the table. The students clustered round as the director showed them what to do.

"Sort through all the decorated fragments," he began. "Separate out the sherds large enough to tell us the shape of the original vessel they came from, pieces with handles, and so on."

The students started on the large piles in bewildered silence. "There seem to be so many different designs," complained one beginner.

"Just keep going," admonished the director. "Once you've sorted through fifty or sixty sherds, you'll find that some fairly obvious categories emerge."

And so it proved. Twenty minutes later, a group of three students asked for advice. "Now we're getting some categories," they cried. "Are we making too many categories?"

The director leaned over the six or seven piles. His experienced eye darted over the sherds, his nimble hands caressing a few particular designs. "Let's see now," he murmured. "You've got about seventy potsherds sorted out. This pile bears black-painted designs, this heap has red-painted panels. Your third and fourth categories both have incised lines on them, but one group are from spouted vessels, the other from flat, shallow platters. All of the groups except one have gray, fine clay, this last a coarse paste. And there are several different vessel forms with red- and black-painted decoration. What you've picked out are a series of easily identified features — decoration, shape, clay type and so on. Keep on doing this but see if you can identify even more features than these few—shapes, decorative styles, and so on."

The three students continued to pore over the sherds. They divided up their initial piles into even more minute categories — black-painted bands with panels of decoration, similar vessels with bands of black, and so on. Once they had sorted through their one hundred and fifty potsherds, they ended up with over twenty piles of sherds, each with different decorations, colors, shapes, clays, or separate combinations of each. By this time, too, every group of workers had done much the same. Students were going from group to group comparing piles. The director listened to the buzz of conversation and decided to intervene.

"O.K., gather round," he said. "You've all sorted out your potsherds into broad groupings. You've done so by identifying different features like shape and decoration. We call these features **attributes.** Now attributes are selected quite arbitrarily. They may be certain measurements, decorative styles, or vessel shapes (see Figure 2.4). A single potsherd may have a turned-out lip, a band of stamped decoration, and a red-painted surface. The clay could be coarse, with a bright red color and a polished interior surface. All of these individual characteristics are attributes. You must make note of as many attributes as you feel you can. Some of these will be used to classify the artifacts into different types."

The director paused for questions. When no one raised a hand, he continued. "Let's take the attributes identified by these two groups on my left. How many attributes did you find? What are they?"

In a few minutes a list of forty attributes appeared on the blackboard. These were decorative motifs, paint colors and clay textures, spouts, bowls, even repair holes in the clay where a crack had been lashed together. The director perused the list.

"Obviously," he went on, "we'll refine the list and expand it as we study the entire collection, but notice how some of the attributes are already forming groups. For example, all our black-painted sherds decorated in rectangular panels come from shallow platters. None of the big, globular pots are made of anything but very coarse clay. Herein lies the problem. What do these apparent groupings of attributes, and many less obvious ones, mean? Are these associations of attributes sheer coincidence or a reflection of actual categories of clay vessels actually used and identified by their makers? Above all, can we use these attribute associations to identify different **types** of vessel (Figure 7.1)? Clearly, all this identification of attributes has as its ultimate purpose identifying types of vessel."

Everyone nodded in agreement. "The next stage is to compile a comprehensive attribute list based on the entire collection. We'll do this by comparing everyone's groupings and discussing them in the light of the attribute list already on the board." The director paused for emphasis.

"But remember one thing," he added. "Where we go from here depends on the attributes we select at this stage. Are we going to look closely at the function of the vessels, at the ways in which their makers used them, or are we more concerned with stylistic variation as a basis for classifying the pots? When we look at the ways attributes vary, we are going to have to think this through rather carefully."

Natural Types

The next day the team assembled in the laboratory to find the director immersed in the attribute list.

"All right," he said. "Now we've got the main attributes sorted out. What about the actual pottery types?"

"It seems pretty obvious to me," said Steve, a young graduate student fresh from his first dig. "These black-painted sherds all come from round-based pots, and that pile of fragments with red panels consists of shallow bowls. It seems that decorative styles coincide with vessel shapes whose attributes tell us what they were used for. The bowls were the ideal shape for eating vegetables or stews, while the round-based pots must have held water or beer. Why don't we call them two types — eating bowls and water storage pots?"

"Wait a minute," interrupted Kathy, a more advanced student. "You can't go that far."

"Why not?" asked Steve. "It seems obvious enough what my two types were used for."

FIGURE 7.1 An archaeologist's type description of a pottery type from South Dakota, "Colombe Collared Rim." This description appears exactly as it was published in 1954 by D. J. Lehmer. This example will give you an idea of the detail required for type description. Do not be dismayed if you do not understand some of the technical terms used; they are irrelevant to the main discussion of types in this text.

Tempering   Grit, diameters ranging from − 0.5 to 2.0 mm. The appearance and composition (quartz, mica, and a little feldspar) suggest that the tempering material is a decomposed granite.

Texture   Medium to coarse.

Hardness   3.0–4.0.

Color   Tan to dark gray; exterior surfaces often heavily carboned.

FORM

Overall shape   Jars with collared rims, constricted necks, rounded shoulders, and rounded bottoms.

Lip   Rounded, occasionally thickened by the addition of a small bracing fillet on the exterior surface.

Rim   All the rims are collared. The collars range from 24 to 55 mm. in height. Interior and exterior profiles are more or less parallel to each other, forming a straight or concave plane which extends downward and outward from the lip. The lower edge of the collar is marked by a fairly abrupt shoulder which forms the junction between the collar and the low curved neck. The bottom of the collar is sometimes scalloped. Below the neck, the vessel wall turns outward toward the shoulder. These rims might be contrasted with the rims of the Foreman types by describing them as Z-rims rather than S-rims, since the surface is flat or concave rather than convex.

Neck   A relatively low, constricted zone below the shoulder of the rim.

Shoulder   Rounded.

Base   Rounded.

HANDLES   One sherd has a short tablike lug extending down from the lower edge of the collar in the same plane as the face of the collar itself. Two others have fractured areas which seem to indicate the presence of loop handles running from the base of the rim collar to the shoulder of the vessel.

SURFACE FINISH   Bodies simple stamped, some with extensive plain areas. The stamping on one of the restored vessels is vertical. Necks are plain or brushed vertically; interior surfaces are plain.

DECORATION   The decoration is confined to the rim and lip. It is preponderantly cord impressed. Patterns consist of a series of horizontal lines, or a series of interlocking triangles filled alternately with horizontal and diagonal cord impressions. The cord-impressed zone is sometimes bordered by a series of punctations. Two pieces were decorated with diagonal broad-trailed lines, and one was plain except for a series of punctations at the base of the rim.

REMARKS   A number of the pieces assigned to Colombe Collared Rim at the Phillips Ranch site show a considerable similarity to some Lower Loup sherds from Nebraska. The most striking difference is in the incised decoration on the Nebraska pieces and the predominantly cord-impressed decoration on the Phillips Ranch rims.

FROM: D. J. Lehmer, *Archaeological Investigations in the Oahe Dam Area, South Dakota, 1950–51,* Bureau of American Ethnology, Bulletin 158, 1954.

"You think it is," replied Kathy. "What you are doing is projecting your own ideas of how the vessels should be used onto the potsherds. You think this bowl would be best used for eating. Why? Because our own culture uses bowls for eating stew. How do you know that the original makers had the same uses for the vessels? They could have used them in a rain dance for all you know! Since we can't talk to the makers, we've got to use some more independent classification, one that avoids our own cultural biases."

"Kathy's right," said the director after a pause in which everybody looked at the sherds again. "Steve succumbed to a common temptation. He used his own cultural experience to classify the bowls and pots into what are known as **natural** or **functional types.** Certainly, every prehistoric society had ideas about the 'right' design for artifacts. Each had its own definite expectations as to the appearance of its masks or choppers. But do these cultural norms coincide with ours? Are modern archaeologists' natural types similar to the actual classifications developed by the makers of the artifacts? Unfortunately, so many variables act on the ways people make their tools that the two often do not coincide. So we've got to come up with some other form of type."

"You've done this before, Nancy," the director continued, turning to a quiet graduate student at the other end of the table. "How do we get away from Steve's natural types?"

Analytical Types

"Well," Nancy began, "I think we should try to create some quite arbitrary groupings of pot types, which concentrate on the stylistic attributes of the potsherd that we all observe (Figure 7.1). After all, our only concern in classifying the pots into types is to compare our material with what's in the sites in the next valley."

"You mean using **analytical** or **stylistic types**?" asked the director.

"Yes," said Nancy. "A series of precisely defined analytical types will define the average specimen within each type and also indicate the approximate range of variation as well."

"How would you do it?" inquired Steve.

"By **convenience typing,**" Nancy continued. "I've worked

with people who have developed analytical types by using their instinct and experience along with arbitrary judgment. They used convenient and conspicuous stylistic features like the shape of a handle or some other obvious physical attribute. It seemed to work quite well."

Steve pounced. "Aren't you assuming that everyone handling the same collection will be able to duplicate your convenience classification by picking out the same attributes?"

"That's true," said Nancy.

"Well, I heard Professor Williams complaining the other day that he couldn't get Jack Foster's published classification of the Acorn site artifacts to agree with his own analysis of the same collection," Steve said triumphantly. "Surely these types are no better than natural ones."

The director intervened. "You're partly right, Steve. There *is* a problem with analytical types, especially if they are poorly defined. It *is* difficult to duplicate other peoples' results. Furthermore, analytical types are normally set up on the basis of several attributes that indicate how the artifact was made, or its shape or decoration. They tend to define an *average* artifact rather than measure the range of variation. As you all must realize, the variation between different artifacts is more important than the average for our purposes."

Attribute Clusters

"We are discussing a classic problem," the director continued. "The researches of the past twenty years have produced enormous quantities of new archaeological data, so much so that it is a full-time job keeping track of the thousands of artifacts from old and new sites. Fortunately, the digital computer and new statistical techniques can be used to store information in computer data banks and to identify patterns of attributes displayed by thousands of individual artifacts. We could use a computer listing of attributes from these potsherds to tell us what percentage of black-painted sherds come from round-based pots with straight rims. Statistical tests could be used to determine if these attribute patterns are significant or not.

"I'm planning to use a new definition of **type,** one that reflects the way **clusters** of attributes seem to pattern repeatedly into regular groups. For example, we may find that sixty of these black-painted sherds are found on pot fragments, while only ten are on bowls, and these latter all have black-painted bird motifs on them. The key word here is **pattern,** for we will be examining clusters of attributes and their associations with each other on hundreds of potsherds."

"How will we know if these clusters mean anything?" asked Kathy.

"By statistical testing," replied the director. "If the distribution of the attributes tests out as being other than a chance one, then the cluster is sometimes the result of the deliberate behavior of the makers. In other words, we may be looking at actual artifact clusters developed by the original manufacturer. Of course, even this approach is dependent on the attributes you initally select to cluster. If you selected attributes that reflect the actual function of the vessel, you could theoretically come out with 'natural types.' "

There was an awed silence.

"Where do we start?" asked Nancy at last.

"We start by reading a paper by Albert Spaulding, who has spent years studying this problem," replied the director (see "Further Reading"). "Then we'll sit down and develop an attribute list and record all the attributes on our sherds. After that, we go to the computer people and get advice on a suitable program for our needs. And once all that is done, we should be able to define some artifact clusters. So let's get to work."

Months later, the research team emerged with a series of artifact clusters they could compare with other clusters from neighboring sites.

UNITS OF ORDERING

The artifact clusters that formed our research team's types all came from a single assemblage. You recall from Chapter 4 that an assemblage is the diverse group of artifacts found together which reflects the shared activities of a community. This assemblage was found in a single site. You recall too that the site is the fundamental unit for all stratigraphic studies in archaeology. If time has passed, one can assume that at least some culture change has taken place at a site.

Many archaeological sites, like the small campsites at Olduvai Gorge, were occupied but once. They consist of a single assemblage of artifacts and a single component — another arbitrary archaeological unit (Figure 7.2). A **component** is a large set of specific cultural features, including such things as a particular pottery design, that serve to distinguish the culture of the inhabitants of a particular occupation level. Sites occupied many times, like Hogup Cave in Utah, contain many components, each of them distinguished by a set of characteristic cultural features that separate them in time and space from other levels at the same site. The social equivalent of the archaeologist's component is the **community.**

Once our research team's analysis is completed, they may find they have only one component to deal with. If the site was occupied several times, they might have two or three. How do they compare these components with those from other, nearby sites? And how do they develop a sequence of occupation levels and cultures for their local area?

When all the artifact collections from the local area have been analyzed and classified to everyone's satisfaction, they are ordered in space and time with the aid of stratigraphic observations, seriation, cross dating, and the use of radiocarbon or tree-ring dates. We described both seriation and cross dating in Chapter 3, techniques that place artifacts in chronological order, with the help of battleship curves and dated components. Figure 7.2 shows how our team joined ten sites into a local sequence, a chronological ordering built up from several multicomponent sites and some single-component settlements within the area. Additionally, they were able to obtain some radiocarbon dates to give an accurate chronology for the sequence.

When the team studied the distribution of their sites, they discovered that two different dated components were repeated at settlements over a considerable area. These were so well dated and precisely distributed in time that two phases in the sequence could be identified.

A phase is a cultural unit like a component and is made up of similar components on different sites. Instead of occuring at only one site, it is found at many settlements, though always within a well-defined chronological bracket. The characteristic artifacts of the phase may be found over hundreds of miles within the area covered by a local sequence. Many archaeologists use the term culture in the same sense as

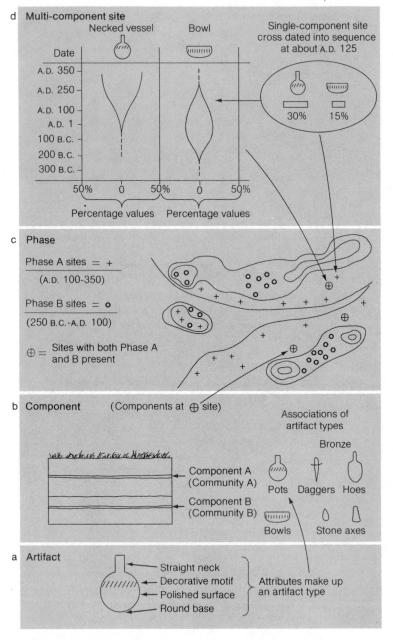

d Multi-component site

Necked vessel

Bowl

Single-component site cross dated into sequence at about A.D. 125

Date

A.D. 350
A.D. 250
A.D. 100
A.D. 1
100 B.C.
200 B.C.
300 B.C.

50%   0   50%   0   50%

Percentage values   Percentage values

30%   15%

c Phase

Phase A sites = +
(A.D. 100-350)

Phase B sites = o
(250 B.C.-A.D. 100)

⊕ = Sites with both Phase A and B present

b Component   (Components at ⊕ site)

Associations of artifact types

Bronze

Component A
(Community A)

Component B
(Community B)

Pots   Daggers   Hoes

Bowls   Stone axes

a Artifact

Straight neck
Decorative motif
Polished surface
Round base

Attributes make up an artifact type

FIGURE 7.2   Archaeological units in use. (a) Patterns of attributes form an artifact type. (b) Cross section through a hypothetical archaeological site with two stratified components. The two components are radiocarbon dated to between 250 B.C. and A.D. 100 and between A.D. 100 and 350 respectively. Our artifact type is a diagnostic vessel in Component A, the later one. The total artifact content from the site is the assemblage. (c) Now the archaeologists have studied dozens of sites in their archaeological region, which consists of an estuary with an offshore island. Higher ground with pine forest overlooks the estuary. When they plotted site distributions, they found that the earlier, Phase B sites were distributed on the higher ground, while the later components were established near the shore where shellfish were abundant. Only three sites contain both components, stratified one above the other. The two distributions are distinctive, both phases defined in space and time, forming a local sequence. (d) At the four two-component sites, the archaeologists seriated the pottery types and other artifacts and obtained distinctive battleship curves. Then they were able to fit other sites into the same sequence by cross dating.

phase. Both are arbitrary terms designed to assist in the ordering of artifacts in time and space. Phases or cultures are normally named after a key site where characteristic artifacts are found. For example, the Acheulian culture is named after the French town of St. Acheul, where the stone axes so characteristic of this culture are found (see Figure 5.1).

Larger Archaeological Units

After many seasons' work, our research team may have studied several local sequences and may be able to describe their finds in a wider context. There are dozens of local sequences within the southwestern United States, for example. Some characteristic art styles or artifacts, like, for example, the Chavín art style that flourished in Peru between 900 B.C. and 200 B.C., spread over enormous distances (Figure 7.3). Archaeologists have developed a number of larger-scale archaeological units to cover such situations. Perhaps the most famous of these are the technological stages of prehistory developed by the Danish archaeologist Christian Jurgensen Thomsen in 1806. His Stone Age, Bronze Age, and Iron Ages are technological labels still in wide use. For information on these and other larger-scale archaeological units, you should consult the "Further Reading" section at the end of this book.

FIGURE 7.3   A Chavín carving on a pillar in the temple interior at
Chavín de Huantar, Peru.

Explanatory Ordering

Our ordering of archaeological data is a descriptive process. It highlights the patterning and regularities existing in
archaeological data. The concepts and units set forth above
are purely descriptive devices used to organize data as a preliminary to studying culture change. These classificatory
units put artifacts and other culture traits into a context of

time and space developed by use of distribution maps, stratigraphy, seriation and cross dating, and chronometric dating methods.

So far we have talked of components, phases, and other units as phenomena in isolation. We have assumed that the artifacts they contain reflect gradual, evolutionary change in human society. But the archaeological record does not invariably reflect an orderly and smooth chronicle of culture change. A radical, new artifact inventory may suddenly appear in components at eight sites, while earlier toolkits suddenly vanish. The economy of sites in a local sequence may change completely within a century as the plow revolutionizes agricultural methods. Such changes are readily observed in thousands of local sequences all over the world. But how did these changes come about? What processes of cultural change were at work to cause major and minor alterations in the archaeological record? It is at this point that the archaeologist turns from description of the past to explanation — to the study of cultural process.

CULTURAL PROCESS

Cultural process consists of the changes in state in human history. We recognize a number of primary cultural processes that have operated specifically in human prehistory, any one of which can be invoked to account for changes in the archaeological record. These are inevitable variation, cultural selection, invention, diffusion, and migration.

Inevitable Variation and Cultural Selection

Inevitable variation is rather similar to the well-known phenomenon of genetic drift in biology. As people learn the behavior patterns of their society, inevitably some minor differences in learned behavior will appear from generation to generation, which, minor in themselves, accumulate over a long time, especially in isolated populations. The snowballing effect of inevitable variation and slow-moving cultural evolution can be detected in dozens of prehistoric societies. For instance, the Adena and Hopewell cultures of the American Midwest developed more and more complex burial

customs between 500 B.C. and A.D. 300, probably as a result
of gradual trends toward greater complexity in religious belief and rituals. There has been a similar trend toward
greater complexity in human culture since the earliest times.
The simple stone choppers of the first humans are the ultimate ancestors of the sophisticated electric carving knife of
today. It is the *rate* of inevitable variation, technological invention, population exchange, and the spread of new ideas
that has accelerated so rapidly since the first choppers were
made.

Cultural selection may involve deliberate choices by a society which recognizes that certain culture changes or inventions may be of advantage. Presumably, for example, many
hunter-gatherer societies deliberately took up agriculture
once they saw the advantages it gave other neighboring peoples who had already adopted the new economies.

Invention

Invention is the creation or evolution of a new idea. Many
inventions, such as new social institutions or religious beliefs leave no trace in the archaeological record. But some
innovations are reflected in new types of surviving artifacts,
such as the plow, or an iron axe. If an invention like plowing
is sufficiently useful to be attractive to more than a few people, the new idea or a product of the idea will spread widely,
and often rapidly.

Archaeologists have studied ways in which inventions
spread by tracing the distribution of distinctive artifacts like
plowshares from their place of origin. The earliest occurrence
of ironmaking, for example, is in northern Turkey about 1500
B.C. Iron tools first appear in the archaeological record of Europe and Egypt very much later. Since the earliest dated iron
artifacts occur in Turkey, we cay say that ironmaking was
invented there.

In the early days of archaeology, people assumed that metallurgy and other major inventions were invented in only
one place — in many cases, the Near East. These innovations then spread all over the world as other societies realized how important the new ideas were. But as importance
of environment and adaptation in the development of human culture have become better understood, this simple

view of invention has been rejected. Agriculture, for example, is now known to have developed quite independently in the Near East, Southeast Asia, Mesoamerica, and Peru. Identical adaptive processes occurred in all these areas. Scholars now try to identify the many and complex interacting factors that caused people to modify their life-styles to adopt food production. The genius of humanity was that it recognized opportunities when they came along and adapted to new circumstances. The issue is not who first cultivated the corn cob but rather to study the dozens of major and minor alterations in human culture that were the result of adaptive changes over time.

Diffusion

Diffusion is the spread of ideas, over long or short distances. Ideas like, for example, a new religious belief are transmitted from individual to individual and ultimately from group to group. But the spread of ideas does not involve actual movements of people. A clear distinction must be made between the spread of abstract ideas like religious beliefs and the spread of material goods, however. The clas-

FIGURE 7.4 The spread of a culture trait in time and space: the cone effect. "The spread of ideas does not involve actual movements of people."

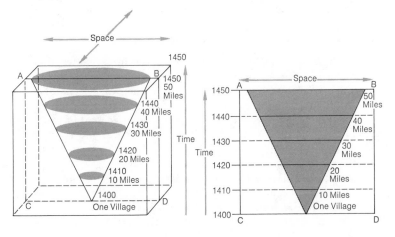

sic example is that of the Hopi Indians of the Southwest.
They received American trade goods but still retained their
own culture, trading objects but rejecting the ideas of an
alien culture.

Let us say that a new type of painted pot is invented in a
single village in A.D. 1400. The advantages of this new vessel
are such that villagers ten miles away learn about it at a beer
party five years later. Within ten years, their potters are
making similar receptacles. Within a short time the pot form
is found commonly in villages ten miles further away. Half a
century later, communities in a fifty-mile radius are making
the now well-established vessel design. If we put this stir-
ring tale on paper, we end up with the cone effect shown
in Figure 7.4. The cone effect is the type of distribution
we study when identifying diffusion in the archaeological
record.

Archaeologically, diffusion is difficult to identify unless
one can use very distinctive artifacts of obvious common origin, demonstrate that the artifacts were invented only in one
place, and trace the distribution of the artifact in space and
time from its origin point to neighboring areas. This means
establishing that the tool was first made in one place and
that other sites nearby are later (Figure 7.4). Instances of diffusion in prehistory are commonplace. A classic example is
the Chavín art style of Peru that diffused widely over the
lowlands from a homeland on the highlands, where it appeared in about 900 B.C.

Migration

Migration involves movements of entire societies that
make a deliberate decision to expand their sphere of influence. English settlers moved to North America, taking their
own culture with them. Spanish conquistadors occupied
Mexico. Migration involves not only the movement of ideas
but a mass shift of people that results in social and cultural
changes on a large scale. A classic prehistoric migration was
that of the Polynesians, who deliberately voyaged from island to island. In each case, new land masses were found by
purposeful exploration, then colonized by small numbers of
people who moved to an uninhabited island.

These types of mass migration are rare in prehistoric

times. They would be reflected in the archaeological record by totally new components and phases or by skeletons of a totally new physical type. To be proved, the migration would have to show up as similar breaks in the cultural sequence at many sites in neighboring local sequences.

A second type of migration is on a smaller scale, when a group of foreigners move into another region and settle there as an organized group. A group of Oaxacans did just that at Teotihuacán in the Valley of Mexico. When René Millon mapped the whole of this remarkable city, he found a concentration of distinctive Oaxacan artifacts in a single residential area. This Oaxacan colony flourished for centuries in an alien city. In this and many other cases, the immigrants adopt some features of the host culture but retain their own cultural identity.

There are other types of migration, too. Slaves and artisans are often unorganized migrants, sometimes taking new technological devices with them. Great warrior migrations, like those of Zulu regiments in South Africa in the early nineteenth century, can cause widespread disruption and population shifts. Such migrations leave few traces in archaeological sites. Within a few generations, the warriors settle down and adopt the sedentary life of the conquered. Only a few new weapon forms reveal the presence of strangers.

Cultural Ecology and Cultural Process

As is obvious, much data is needed to identify invention, diffusion, or migration in the archaeological record. The *identification* of these classic cultural processes is largely a mechanical, descriptive activity because the artifacts used, be they stone axes, pots, or swords, are considered in isolation, and not as an element of the total cultural system of which they are part. The *explanation* of culture change requires more sophisticated research models, ones based on the notion that human cultural systems are made up not only of many complex interacting elements — religious beliefs, technology, subsistence, and so on — but that these cultural systems also interact with the natural environment and other complex systems.

Cultural ecology is a means of studying human culture that gives a picture of the way in which human populations adapt to, and transform, their environments. Human cultural systems have to adapt to other cultures and also to the natural environment. So many factors influence cultural systems, indeed, that the processes by which cultural similarities and differences are generated are not easy to understand. Cultural ecologists see human cultures as subsystems interacting with other major subsystems, among them the biotic community and the physical environment. Thus, the key to understanding cultural process lies in understanding the interactions between these various subsystems. Human culture is, ecologically speaking, the way in which humans compete successfully with other animals, plants, and other humans. But even though the number of probable adaptations to a specific environment is limited, human responses to different environments will be different and distinctive. Thus, communities with highly distinctive cultures may occupy the same or similar environments.

Many archaeologists have started to use cultural ecology to hypothesize about major developments in world prehistory like the origins of agriculture and civilization. Kent Flannery, for example, has argued that a whole set of complex variables — economic, technological, religious, social, and environmental — affected the behavior of the first Sumerian city-dwellers in Mesopotamia. Trade did not cause urban life, nor did religious beliefs alone, he argues. What one has to look for is the ways in which societies of the time regulated cultural change, the numerous interlocking checks and balances that encouraged and discouraged culture change. Many of these factors are intangible ideas or values that are hard to find in an archaeological site.

In the study of cultural process, the ultimate objective is to establish the rules by which a society ordered itself and permitted cultural change. We have only to look at our own society to see how many roadblocks can lie in the way of even simple changes in our way of living. In the pages that follow, we look at some of the ways in which archaeologists have tried to look at intangible parts of prehistoric cultural systems.

8

SUBSISTENCE

> There was a noise, and behold a shaking, and the
> bones came together, bone to his bone.
> And when I beheld, lo, the sinews and the flesh
> came up upon them, and the skin covered them
> above, but there was no breath in them.
>
> EZEKIEL 37: 7–8

We now consider one of the most fascinating questions in archaeology: how did prehistoric peoples make their living? Once archaeologists realized that human prehistory was the story of humanity's diverse and constantly changing adaptations to world environments, they could not afford to ignore prehistoric subsistence activities, the ways in which people had fed themselves and achieved a satisfactory diet.

When studying prehistoric subsistence, the archaeologist seeks to answer many fundamental questions, among them these: What was the role of domestic animals in a mixed farming economy? How important was fishing to a shellfish-oriented population living by the ocean? Was a particular site occupied seasonally while the inhabitants concentrated on, say, bird snaring, to the exclusion of all other subsistence activities? What agricultural systems were used? How was the land cultivated? This chapter reviews some of the ways in which we seek the answers to these and other related subsistence questions.

EVIDENCE FOR SUBSISTENCE

The archaeological evidence for prehistoric subsistence consists of artifacts and food remains. How much survives

132

is, of course, dependent on the soil and climatic conditions. All too often the evidence for ancient diet is incomplete. While stone axes or iron hoe blades may give an indication of hunting or agriculture, they hardly yield the kind of detail archaeologists need. Many important artifacts used in the chase or for agriculture were made from perishable materials like bone, wood, or fiber (Figure 8.1).

Food remains themselves survive very unevenly. Animal bones are the most common economic data, while birds, fish, and remains of invertebrates like beetles and frogs are not uncommon. Vegetal remains are normally underrepresented.

PREHISTORIC DIET

The ultimate aim of studying prehistoric food remains is not only to establish how people obtained their food, but to reconstruct their actual diet as well. An overall picture of prehistoric diet involves, of course, developing a comprehensive picture of all food resources available to the people and then answering such questions as these: What proportion of the diet was meat? How diverse were dietary sources? Did the principal diet sources change from season to season? Was food stored? These and many other questions can be answered only from composite pictures of prehistoric diet reconstructed from many sources of evidence.

FIGURE 8.1   A reconstructed stone axe used by early Danish farmers for forest clearance. Such artifacts tell us little about prehistoric economic practices.

Just occasionally, however, it is possible to gain insights into actual meals consumed thousands of years ago. The stomach of Tollund man, whose body was buried and preserved in a Danish peat bog, contained the remains of a finely ground porridge made from barley, linseed, and several wild grasses (see Figure 5.2). No meat was found in his belly. Human droppings (coprolites or feces) found in dry caves in the United States and Mexico have been analyzed under fine microscopes. The inhabitants of Lovèlock Cave in the central Nevada desert were eating bullrush and cattail seeds, as well as fish-like Lahontan chub from the waters of nearby Humboldt Lake. These fish were eaten raw or roasted over a fire. One coprolite contained the remains of at least fifty-one chub, calculated by a fish expert to represent a total fish weight of 3.65 pounds. The same people were eating adult and baby birds, as well as water tiger beetles. Human droppings from Texas caves near the mouth of the Pecos River have been subjected to pollen analyses so precise that the investigators established the sites to have been occupied regularly during the spring and summer months between 800 B.C. and A.D. 550, a period of thirteen hundred years.

Although coprolite studies are a promising source of dietary information, the food remains from most sites are far too incomplete to allow more than a very general impression of total diet. Let us now look at some of the major sources of information on prehistoric subsistence surviving in archaeological sites.

ANIMAL BONES

Broken animal bones can tell us a great deal about ancient hunting, herd management, and butchery practices. One can identify different mammal species from their skeletal remains. Unfortunately, however, most animal bones found in archaeological sites have been smashed literally to ribbons by the inhabitants. Every piece of usable meat is stripped from the bones of even the smallest animals or the portions of larger mammals brought back to the settlement. Sinews are made into thongs. Skins become clothing, containers, or even part of a shelter. Even the entrails are eaten. The hunters smash the bones themselves to get at the marrow or for manufacture into arrowheads or other tools. The fragmentation of animal bones results from many domestic activities, quite apart from trampling underfoot and scavenging by dogs and carnivores. Thus, the archaeologist is faced with the formidable task of identifying the animal that was hunted or kept by the site's inhabitants from tiny, discarded fragments. Further, the role the animal played in the economy, diet, and culture of the community must be assessed.

Animal Bone Analysis

Most animal bone collections consist of thousands of scattered fragments from all parts of a site. Occasionally, however, a kill site, like prehistoric bison kills on the Great Plains or the carcasses of big game slaughtered by early humans in East Africa, provides a chance to reconstruct the hunters' activities in greater detail. Apart from such unusual finds, most collections have to be sorted out in the laboratory simply to give a general impression of hunting and stock raising at the site.

The first stage in bone analysis is to isolate the diagnostic fragments. Only a few bones are normally identifiable. One three-thousand-year-old central African hunting camp yielded only 2,128 identifiable fragments out of a total of 195,415 bones! The actual identifications are made by comparing such diagnostic body parts as the teeth, jaws, horns, and some limb bones with modern animal skeletons (Figure 8.2). This process is not as easy as it sounds. Domestic sheep and goats, for example, have skeletons that are almost identical to those of their wild ancestors. The bones of the domestic ox closely resemble those of the African buffalo, and so on. But accurate identifications are vital, for they provide answers to many questions. Are both domestic and wild animals present? If so, what are the proportions of each group? Were the inhabitants concentrating on a single species to the exclusion of all others? Are any now-extinct species present?

Game Animals

A collection of game animals yields a wealth of information about the wide variety of mammals that ancient hunters killed with astonishingly simple weapons. North American

FIGURE 8.2 At the top, a dog skeleton showing the most important body parts from the bone identification point of view. At the bottom, a domestic ox jaw seen from above showing the characteristic cusp patterns of molars and premolars that erupt in order as the beast gets older.

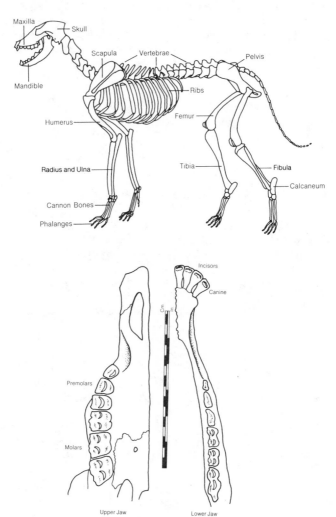

Paleo-Indian bands used game drives, spears, and other weapons to hunt herds of now-extinct big game. So effective were early American hunters that some zoologists believe much Plains big game to have become extinct at least in part as a result of overhunting. Four hundred thousand years ago, Spanish hunter-gatherer bands cooperated with one another in pursuit of herds of huge elephants and bison, whose bones litter their campsites.

When the identified game animal bones are counted, one species may appear to dominate the collection. Many hunters tend to concentrate on a single species, whether from economic necessity, convenience, or cultural preference. But the dominance can be misleading, for many societies restrict the hunting of particular animals. Others forbid males or females to eat certain species, while others may be consumed by everyone. The !Kung San of the Kalahari today have a complicated set of personal, and age- or sex-specific taboos to regulate their eating habits. No one may eat all the twenty-nine game animals regularly taken by the San. Indeed, no two individuals will have the same set of taboos. Such complicated restrictions are repeated with innumerable variations in other hunter-gatherer societies. So the simple figure of, say, 40 percent white-tailed deer and 20 percent wild geese may, in fact, reflect a much more complex set of behavioral variables than mere concentration on two species.

Domesticated Animals

Domestic animal bones present even more difficulties. Owners can affect their herds and flocks in many ways — by selective breeding to improve meat yields or to increase wool production, and by regulating the ages at which they slaughter surplus males and old animals. All domesticated animals originated from wild species with an inclination to be sociable, a characteristic that aided close association with humans. Animal domestication may have begun when a growing human population needed a regular food supply to support a greater density of people per square mile. Wild animals lack many characteristics valuable in their domestic relatives. Wild sheep have hairy coats, but their wool is unsuitable for spinning. The ancestors of oxen and domestic goats produced milk for their young, but not enough for human consumption. People have bred wild animals selectively over long periods to develop special characteristics. Often the resulting domestic animals can no longer survive in the wild.

The history of domestic animals has to be written from fragmentary animal bones found in sites occuped by prehistoric farmers. The difference between domestic and wild animal bones is often so small that it is often virtually impossible to tell the two apart. No one can tell a domestic sheep or goat from a wild one on the basis of a single jaw. One has to work with large numbers of animals, studying changing body sizes as the animals undergo selective breeding. Early Near Eastern sheep, for instance, are smaller and display less size variation than their wild relatives. Even then, it is, in the words of the Scriptures, "difficult to tell the sheep from the goats."

Aging and Butchery

Prehistoric peoples hunted game animals for food or kept domestic herds for meat, plowing, riding, or for their milk. Both hunter-gatherers and farmers had some preferences for young, tender meat from younger animals.

Some preferences can be detected by studying fragmentary bones found in archaeological sites. Age can be worked out by examining teeth wear. If molars are heavily worn, and the teeth fully erupted from the jaw, then chances are the animal is fully grown and past its prime (Figure 8.2). Younger animals often have limb bones with only partially joined ends. Some Near Eastern sites have yielded such large bone collections that it has been possible to study the unfused limb bones of goats and show that some early farming communities began to kill their domestic goats at a younger age than wild ones. Perhaps this changing preference is a sign of increased reliance on goat herding rather than hunting.

Butchery pattern can tell us more, too. Hunter-gatherers may have had a preference for animals in their prime, but the farmer has other considerations. Any herd of sheep, goats, or cattle has a large reservoir of males surplus to breeding requirements. Some may be castrated and then used for riding and dragging carts or plows. But even with these outlets, the surplus males represent an abundant source of wealth and prime meat on the hoof. Many prehistoric farming societies often redistributed their wealth through the community at weddings and other ceremonial occasions, when the owner's social obligations were satisfied through reduction of his herd surplus.

Butchering the carcass of even a moderate-sized animal can be a lengthy task. There is no doubt that prehistoric butchers were skillful meat dressers. The great archaeologist Louis Leakey took pride in demonstrating how easy it was to dismember an antelope with a stone blade. We can study prehistoric butchery practices by plotting artifact and bone patterns found on kill sites, where the remains of the butchered animals were finally abandoned by the hunters. The Olsen-Chubbuck site, in Colorado, was the location of a mass game drive eight thousand years ago, a hunt that took a small herd of bison to their death in a narrow arroyo. Archaeologists have determined that for several days the hunters camped by their prey as they dismembered the uppermost bison in the confused heap of dead animals before them. When they had eaten and dried enough meat, they simply walked away and left the rotting carcasses for archaeologists to find thousands of years later.

The Olsen-Chubbuck bison were far too large for the hunters to take back to camp. But much prehistoric game meat came from smaller creatures which were carried to base and then dismembered at leisure. In this case, they may be overrepresented in the bone collection. So many factors affect the counts of identified bones from any collection of animal remains that one has to interpret the fragments in the context of artifact patterns and all other sources of data with potential bearing on the behavior of the people who killed the animals.

VEGETABLE REMAINS

Gathering and agriculture are almost invariably unrepresented in most sites, because the tiny seeds and other vegetable remnants that result from such activities as food storage, grinding, and harvesting are among the most fragile of all archaeological remains. Except for occasional burnt seeds found in hearths or storage pits, the vegetable remains from human feces, and grain impressions in clay pot walls, almost all evidence for prehistoric gathering and agriculture comes from dry sites, where preservation conditions are almost perfect (Figure 8.3).

The recovery of such fragile remains requires slow work with fine screens. Some archaeologists have started to use flotation methods to recover thousands of hitherto unrecoverable vegetable remains. With this technique, water or chemicals are used to free tiny seeds from the deposits. The freshly excavated soil is poured into a container and sinks slowly to the bottom while the light seeds float on the sur-

FIGURE 8.3   A grain impression preserved on a clay pot fragment from an early farming site in eastern England. (Approximately 2.2 inches.)

face. Stuart Struever was able to recover 36,000 hickory nut fragments, 4,200 acorn shells, over over 2,000 seeds from other species from ovens, hearths, and pits in the Apple Creek site in the lower Illinois Valley using simple flotation techniques. At the Ali Kosh mound in Iran, Kent Flannery and Frank Hole thought that plant remains were scarce at the site. Then they used flotation methods and recovered 40,000 seeds from their trenches! Flotation methods have begun to revolutionize the study of plant remains, for they provide large seed samples that can be studied with the aid of statistical methods.

Most of our knowledge of early major food crops like wheat, barley, and maize has so far come from dry caves rather than flotation. Richard MacNeish obtained a continuous sequence of human occupation for the period 10,000 years ago to the Spanish Conquest from Tehuacán Valley in Mexico. He dug more than a dozen open sites and caves; all of them so dry they yielded over 80,000 wild plant remains and 25,000 specimens of domestic corn. When the vegetable remains had been identified, MacNeish knew that the inhabitants of Tehuacán were obtaining 18 percent of their food from cultivation of corn and other crops in 5000 B.C., and a third of it from agriculture in 3400 B.C. Fifteen hundred years later, several hybrid varieties of maize were in use and agriculture was far more important than foraging for wild plants. Not only that, but the earliest maize cobs, dating to around 5000 B.C. and earlier, were no more than 0.78 inches long, while later ones were far larger. Unfortunately, MacNeish was unable to identify the original wild ancestor of Tehuacán maize, perhaps a native grass called *teosinte.*

Farmers modify the landscape around them, by grazing their herds and by clearing forests. Simple, shifting cultivation techniques require new garden acreage every season. Each time cultivation required more cleared woodland, drastic environmental changes have been triggered. Few people have ever tried to assess the impact of early agricultural economies on the world environment. Danish botanist Johannes Iversen was able to spot a sharp drop in the percentages of tree pollens in layers of northern European peat bogs dating to about 3000 B.C. The forest trees declined suddenly. At the same time, the number of grass pollens increased sharply. Traces of several cultivation weeds also appeared at the same time. Iversen was able to pin down the moment when farmers first cleared natural forest to make way for their crops.

This early clearance activity dramatizes how very little we know about prehistoric agriculture and gathering, simply because the archaeological evidence is so hard to recover. Our ignorance has led, for example, to the belief that all hunter-gatherers spent their lives in a perennial state of starvation, relieved occasionally by meat-eating orgies. Nothing could be further from the truth. The !Kung San, present-day hunter-gatherer inhabitants of the Kalahari Desert in southern Africa, know of at least eighty-five edible seeds and roots. Most of the time they eat but eight of these. The rest of the vegetable resource base provides a reliable cushion for this hunter-gatherer population in times when key vegetable foods are scarce. Such peoples have a buffer against famine that many farmers with their cleared lands, much higher population densities, and crops that rely on regular rainfall rarely enjoy. Is a farming life really to be preferred? Our glimpses into prehistory suggest this tantalizing question.

BIRDS, FISH, AND MOLLUSKS

Bird bones, although very informative, are often neglected at the expense of larger mammal remains. In 1926, Hildegarde Howard studied a large bird bone collection from an Indian midden on the eastern shores of San Francisco Bay. The inhabitants had hunted many water birds, especially ducks, geese, and cormorants. When Howard looked more closely at the bones, she found that all the geese were migrant winter visitors, which frequent the bay area between January and April. Nearly all the cormorants were immature specimens, birds about five to six weeks old. Had the Indians been raiding cormorant rookeries? Howard consulted rookery records and estimated that the birds had been killed about June 28th. Thus, the site had been occupied both during the winter and early summer, one of many settlements where bird bones give evidence of seasonal occupation.

Fishing, like bird hunting, became more important as people began to specialize in different lifeways and adapt to highly specific environments. Evidence for fishing comes both from artifacts and from fragile fish bones, which, when they survive, can be identified with considerable accuracy.

Freshwater and ocean fish may be caught with nets or with basket-like fish traps. Some Indians who lived on the site of modern Boston in about 2500 B.C. built a dam of vertical stakes and brush. When the Atlantic tides rose, fish were directed into gaps in the dam and trapped in huge numbers. Barbed fish spears and fish hooks are relatively commonplace finds in archaeological sites, but such artifacts tell us little about the importance of fishing in prehistoric subsistence. Did the people fish all the year round, or only when salmon were running? Did they concentrate on coastal species or venture far offshore in large canoes? Such questions can be answered only by examining the actual fish bones themselves.

The Chumash Indians of southern California were remarkably skillful fishermen, who went far offshore in frameless plank canoes to fish with hook and line, basket, net, and harpoon. It was no surprise when the fish bones found on archaeological sites at Century Ranch, Los Angeles, included not only the bones of shallow-water fish like the leopard shark and California halibut, but the remains of albacore, ocean skipjack, and large, deepwater rock fish, species that occur in deep water and can be caught only there. Without the fish bones, no one would have had any idea how effective the maritime adaptation of the Chumash and related groups was. Early Spanish accounts speak of over ten thousand Indians living in the Santa Barbara area of California alone, a large population indeed. Archaeology has shown that this maritime population was able to exploit a very broad spectrum of marine resources.

Fishing, with its relatively predictable food resources and high protein potential, allows much more sedentary settlement than other forms of hunting and gathering. The Northwest Coast Indians enjoyed a very rich maritime culture, based on ocean fishing and salmon runs that enabled considerable numbers of people to live in one area for long periods of time.

Shellfish from seashore, lake, or river have played an important part in prehistoric diet for many thousands of years. Freshwater mollusks were important both to California Indians and to prehistoric peoples living in the southeastern United States. Most mollusks have a limited food value in themselves, so enormous quantities are needed to feed even a small number of people. One estimate for a hundred peoples' mollusk needs for a month runs as high as three tons. In all probability, mollusks were more a supplemental food at certain times of the year than a staple. They were simply too much effort to collect in sufficient quantity.

Even sporadic collecting led to the rapid accumulation of huge piles of shells **(shell middens)** at strategic points on lake or ocean shores, near rocky outcrops or tidal pools where mollusks were commonly found.

Shell midden excavations in California and elsewhere have yielded thousands of shells, which are counted, identified, and also measured to check for size changes. When Claude Warren sampled a shell midden near San Diego, California, he found five major species of shellfish commonly exploited by the inhabitants. The earliest shellfish collectors concentrated on the bay mussel and oysters, both of which flourish on rocky shores. But, by 4000 B.C., the lagoon by the shell middens had silted up to the extent that sand-loving scallops and Venus shells were now collected, for the earlier species were unable to flourish in the new, sandy environment. Soon afterward, however, the lagoon became so clogged that the shellfish collectors moved away, never to return. And their abandoned seashells told the story of the changing environment around the sites.

Both fresh and saltwater shells were widely used as prehistoric ornaments. Gulf Coast shells were bartered over enormous distances of the southeastern and midwestern United States, to peoples who had never seen the ocean. Sometimes such ornaments could assume incredible prestige value. When the nineteenth-century explorer David Livingstone visited Chief Shinte in central Africa in 1855, he found him wearing two seashells that had come over a thousand miles inland from the distant East African coast. The chief told him that two such shells would buy a slave, five a large ivory elephant tusk. Small wonder that enterprising merchants were trading china replicas of these shells in central Africa half a century later!

ROCK ART

Sometimes prehistoric rock art gives a vivid insight into subsistence activities long ago, into hunts and fishing expeditions of the distant past. Hunter-gatherers and fishermen have sometimes left paintings of their daily life behind them on the walls of caves and rockshelters. Careful examination of these paintings can take one back centuries and millennia to the time when the people were killing the animals whose bones lie in the occupation deposits under the observer's feet. Many details of weapons, of domestic equipment, and of hunting and fishing methods can be discerned in these vivid scenes.

The Stone Age paintings of southern Africa have long been famous for their depictions of life in prehistoric times. At Tsoelike River rockshelter in Lesotho, southern Africa, a group of fishermen is depicted assembled in their boats (Figure 8.4). They have cornered a shoal of fish that are

FIGURE 8.4 The fishing scene from Tsoelike rockshelter, Lesotho, southern Africa.

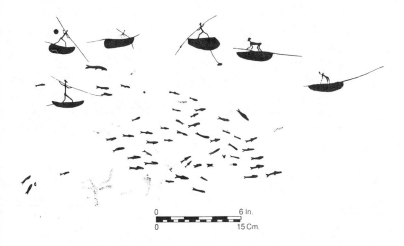

0   6 In.
0   15 Cm.

swimming around in confusion. Some boats have lines that seem to be anchors. The fishermen are busy spearing their quarry. Another famous scene depicts a peacefully grazing herd of ostriches. Among them lurks a hunter wearing an ostrich skin, his legs and bow protruding beneath the belly of the apparently harmless bird. One wonders if his hunt was successful.

The artists painted big game hunts, honey collectors, women gathering fruit, cattle raids, even red-coated British soldiers. Scenes like these take one back to hot days when a small group of hunters pursued their wounded quarry until it weakened and collapsed. The panting hunters have stalked their prey for hours and relax in the shade as they watch its death throes. Then they settle down to butcher the dead animal before carrying the meat and skin home to be shared with their group. Few artifacts survive from actual scenes such as these. But the ultimate objective of reconstructing ancient subsistence patterns is to recreate, from the few patterned traces that have survived in the soil, just such long days in the sun.

9

INTERACTION

> Thus the sum of things is ever being replenished,
> and mortals live one and all by give and take. Some
> races wax and wane, and in a short space the tribes
> of living things are changed and like runners hand
> on the torch of life.
>
> LUCRETIUS, *De Rerum Natura*

The toolkits and food remains found in archaeological sites reflect their inhabitants' material culture and subsistence activities. Hunter-gatherers tend to have portable toolkits, manufactured for the most part from organic materials that do not survive well in archaeological sites (see Figure 4.5). Many of their sites are temporary camps. Only rarely can the archaeologist look at the patterning of artifacts and food remains in such camps, for many are gone forever. But the more sedentary farmer settles in one spot for much longer periods of time and is confronted with a much more elaborate set of annual tasks. The farmer has to store each year's food surplus, too, an activity that adds immediate complexity to a farming settlement. Substantial houses, storage pits, cemeteries, threshing floors, cattle enclosures — all these can be elements in even a small farming village.

Archaeologists study the patterning of structures like houses and storage pits just as thoroughly as they study artifacts and food remains. They also study the distributions in time and space of different communities and the relationships between them. All of these activities are classified under the term **settlement archaeology,** which reveals the many ways in which individual communities relate to one another — through trade, religious beliefs, and social ties, to name some of them.

SETTLEMENT PATTERNS

Settlement patterns are determined by many factors, including environment, economic practices, and technological skills. The distribution of San camps in the Kalahari Desert is dependent on the availability of water supplies and vegetable foods. Ancient Maya settlements in Mexico were laid out in a pattern determined by political and religious organization. Village layout can be determined by the need to protect cattle against lions or raiding parties. Other settlements may be strung out at intervals along an important trade route, like a river. Population growth or increases in herd size are reasons why the capacities of hunting grounds or grazing areas may become overtaxed, in which case new adaptations and alterations in the settlement pattern result. Even the positions of houses are dictated by a complex variety of social, economic, and personal factors that may defy explanation — especially when one has only archaeological evidence to go on.

Settlement archaeology is part of the analysis of human interactions with, and adaptations to, the natural environment. The houses and villages of a prehistoric society, like the artifacts and food residues by their hearths, are part of the settlement pattern. This settlement pattern involves relationships among people who decided — on the basis of practical, political, economic, and social reasons — to place their houses, settlements and religious structures where they did. By studying settlement patterns, we have a chance to examine the intangible factors that caused culture change in prehistory.

Canadian archaeologist Bruce Trigger has recognized three distinct levels of human settlement. The first is the single building; the second, the arrangement of these buildings within a community; the third, the distribution of communities against the landscape. We will examine each of these three levels briefly.

Structures

Human structures exist in infinite variety, all the way from the simple brush shelters of hunter-gatherers to the elaborate villas of Imperial Rome. The pyramids of Gizeh, Maya temples, even cattle pens, are all structures. Both environmental and societal factors, as well as economic considerations, have dictated the design of human structures. Twenty thousand years ago big game hunters on the West Russian plains lived half underground in long houses made of skins and mammoth (arctic elephant) bones. These structures were effective in protecting their inhabitants against cold in a timberless environment. In contrast, tropical African farmers live in areas where the daytime temperatures regularly exceed 100 degrees Fahrenheit and the nights too are hot. So they live much of their lives in the shade of their pole-and-mud huts, whose thatched roofs project far beyond the walls. Grass, puddled mud, or other convenient local raw materials have provided insulation for humankind — whether from summer's heat or arctic cold.

Details of house design are often determined by social and economic considerations. Many societies had standardized house plans, for everyone had the same economic opportunities and the same amount of wealth. The householders carried out various activities at home, activities reflected in the patterning of artifacts in abandoned rooms. Variations in artifact content can reflect different subsistence activities, social status, wealth, and manufacturing skills.

When Kent Flannery and his students excavated a series of farming villages in the Valley of Oaxaca, Mexico, dating to between 1350 and 850 B.C., they not only uncovered and recorded the one-roomed thatched wattle-and-daub-houses, but plotted the associated artifact patterns as well. They distinguished carefully between the house with its contents and the cluster of household storage pits, graves, and garbage heaps that lay nearby. Not only did Flannery plot household features very carefully, he also identified areas where special activities took place from the specialist toolkits — for beadmaking and the like — associated with them. While every household obtained, processed, and stored food, even if the types of food consumed by each varied, some Oaxacan households spent much time making stone tools or ornaments. These specialist activities presumably supplied the needs of the community as a whole. In this Mexican example, and in all studies of individual structures, the artifacts and activities associated with them are just as important to the archaeologist as the design and layout of the structure itself.

Communities

Every household member interacts with other members of the household and also with individuals in other households within the community. And entire households interact with other households as well. Once one begins to look at a community of households, new complexities enter into the picture. The first is that of permanency of settlement, which is affected primarily by the realities of subsistence and ecology. How long San camps are occupied is determined by the availability of water, game, and vegetable foods near the site; the camp moves at regular intervals. In contrast, early city dwellers in Mesopotamia who used irrigation in their fields never had to move their settlement.

The layout of a community is greatly determined by social and political factors, particularly by family and kinship ties. Marriage customs and rules of residence and inheritance may multiply the number of houses associated with a single household. A father may live with his sons in a cattle camp and their families occupy houses within his enclosure. Variables like land ownership may be reflected in community layout, too. The only way archaeologists can study these factors is by looking for patterns of settlement features and artifacts that may reflect kin groups and other social ties.

The largest community settlement pattern ever investigated systematically is that of Teotihuacán, where René Millon has mapped dozens of residential compounds, a market, and vast ceremonial structures (Figure 9.1). He even found a special quarter where foreigners from Oaxaca — revealed by their distinctive pottery — lived in an alien city for centuries. René Millon sought the answers to many questions. What social classes existed in the city? What specialist crafts were practiced and where? How many people lived at Teotihuacán at different periods? The only way to answer such questions was to map the entire city and make comprehensive surface collections and test excavations to give an overall picture of the total settlement pattern.

How can one measure the size of small villages, let alone huge cities like Teotihuacán? While informed guesses are sometimes useful, the only reliable method is to calculate the population on the basis of the number of households in a village at a given moment in its history. And such calcula-

FIGURE 9.1   Teotihuacán, Valley of Mexico, a prehistoric city that was mapped in detail by René Millon. The Pyramid of the Moon is in the foreground; the Avenue of the Dead stretches into the distance; the giant Pyramid of the Sun is to the left of the avenue in the distance. From *Urbanization at Teotihuacán, Mexico*, v.1, pt.1, *The Teotihuacán Map: Text* by René Millon, copyright © 1973 by René Millon, by permission of the author.

tions require large-scale excavations and complex statistical tests. In the case of Teotihuacán, Millon counted rooms and possible sleeping spaces and came up with an intelligent guess of one hundred and twenty-five thousand — a conservative estimate.

If a village is growing, there comes a point when it can grow no further. So some people form a new settlement that flourishes alongside the original village. But sometimes, as in Oaxaca, the villagers continued to live in a steadily growing settlement. Eventually it outgrew its contemporary neighbors. Why did the villagers elect to stay together? Did the larger site survive because its particular location was a favorable one for trade or religious ceremonies? These are the sorts of questions that archaeologists can answer only by looking at site distributions and the resources in their surrounding natural environments. A community does not exist in isolation.

Catchment Areas

Every settlement has a **catchment area** around it, a circular zone of natural resources upon which it can draw. This notion of catchment areas was first developed by geographers studying European peasant agriculture a century ago. The further the resources in an area are from a settlement, the less likely they are to be exploited. Anthropologist Richard Lee found that !Kung San women, for example, are unlikely to forage more than a comfortable day's walk from their village. The village thus has a five-mile-radius catchment area for foraging.

The analysis of site catchment area involves designating a series of concentric circles around the settlement at regular intervals, say of two miles, and then making an inventory of the agricultural land, vegetable foods, game, water supplies, and so on that are available in each circle today. This data is then compared with the excavated finds. Specific questions are asked. For example: from how far away must plant, animal, and mineral resources come? Each artifact, every type of seed, the exotic finds and animal bones, all are located within the site catchment area. Then one can determine which resources came from nearby, which from afar.

Kent Flannery examined the resources he found in excavations at San José Mogote in Oaxaca (1150–850 B.C.). By taking the many seeds found by flotation techniques, the animal bones, mineral resources like clay and salt, and imported objects like seashells, he found that San José Mogote needed a radius of less than one to three miles to satisfy its basic agricultural needs. Today common minerals and seasonal wild vegetable foods are found within the three-mile circle, game meat and construction materials within the nine-mile zone. Exotic trade materials and the requirements of ceremonial life

FIGURE 9.2 (a) Site catchment area around San José Mogote, Valley of Oaxaca. (b) The overlapping catchment zones of villages in the same area.

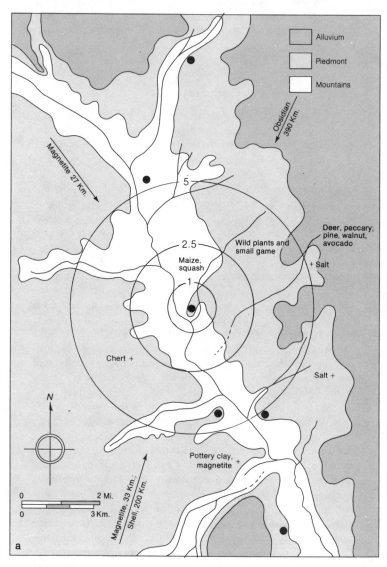

154

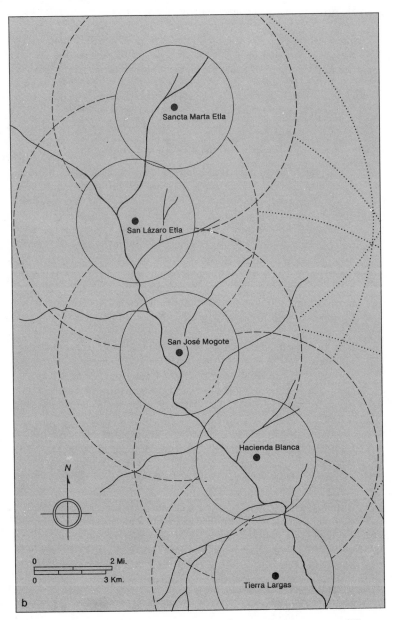

Sancta Marta Etla

San Lázaro Etla

San José Mogote

Hacienda Blanca

Tierra Largas

N

0   2 Mi.

0   3 Km.

b

155

required occasional collecting trips up to thirty miles from the settlement, and some contacts over longer distances. When Flannery plotted the catchment areas of neighboring villages, he found that the one- to three-mile circles of each settlement did not overlap, but the wider ones where minerals and other needs were satisfied did (Figure 9.2). Seasonal camps were built in the outer zones, where every community shared common resources.

Site Interactions and Distributions

Site catchment analysis is really a form of resource inventory, but one that leads us to explore the interactions between different communities. No human being has ever lived in complete isolation, for even the smallest hunter-gatherer family group has at least fleeting contacts with neighboring bands at certain times of the year. But, as human societies become more complex and settlements more permanent, intercommunity relationships become much more complicated. Different settlements depend more and more on one another for essential raw materials, like salt or copper ore, and for specialist products — stone knives, religious ornaments, and the like. Growing villages might split into two settlements that, while separated in space, still maintain close ties of kinship. Human settlement patterns are not just site dots on maps. They are complex and constantly changing networks of human interaction, of trade, religion, and social ties, of differing adaptations to local environmental challenges.

Archaeologists study settlement patterns on this scale by plotting their data on site distribution maps derived from field surveys and aerial photographs. Their ultimate goal is to reconstruct the factors that caused the settlement pattern — now a collection of site dots — in the first place. Of course, any attempt to use a distribution map involves attempts to assess the reliability of the data on the map. Do the painstakingly collected data reflect human actions of the past or merely the earnest guesswork of archaeologists? The process of analyzing distributions and settlement patterns comes under the general heading of **spatial analysis.**

Site Hierarchies

Spatial analysis in archaeology begins with the careful development of a classification of archaeological sites in a region, like that developed by archaeologists working in the Valley of Mexico (Figure 9.3). Each of these site types has a relationship to others, the total distribution of all site types

FIGURE 9.3   A site hierarchy in Mesoamerica. (a) Simplified hierarchy of site types. (b) Hypothetical site hierarchy on the ground, with the major regional center serving secondary centers spaced at regular intervals. These in turn serve larger villages and their networks of hamlets.

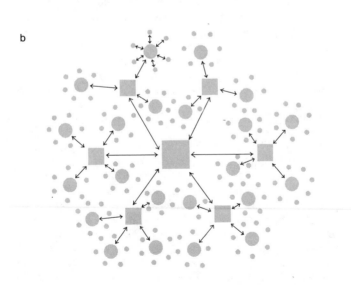

making up a settlement pattern. Each site type is defined by the characteristic structures, artifact patterns, and forms in it. These definitions provide us with a way to organize the sites into a hierarchy of successive levels of settlements. We then need to look at the processes by which the hierarchy arose in the first place.

Central Place Theory

In 1933, the German geographer Walter Christaller developed a series of statements about the relationships between South German towns and the rural communities around them. His ideas, which have become known as **central place theory,** are based on two key assumptions. First, all central places (towns) providing similar services and functions and serving areas of equal size will be spaced at equal distances from each other. This is the most economic spacing possible. And second, a hierarchy of central places will develop, with fewer large places having major facilities than smaller places. The largest places will provide not only the services of smaller centers but also a series of central functions. The smaller centers in turn serve numerous settlements smaller yet. The entire hierarchy is connected by a network of services and relationships.

In Mesoamerica, for example, Christaller would have major Maya ceremonial centers like Tikal servicing a huge area, in which less important centers would be spaced at regular intervals, themselves in turn servicing the villages in their own territories. Every center and minor community would still turn to Tikal for certain unique economic, social, and religious functions.

The concept of a hierarchy of central places is obviously vital to settlement archaeology. It enables one to look at, say, a distribution of Maya ceremonial centers and villages as an interlocking network of settlements. Within this network, the importance of individual sites might wax and wane over time. But the changing settlement picture is encased in a defined larger pattern. This structured network can be traced as it alters through time, by use of data from survey and excavations. Using such a framework, archaeologists can attempt to determine whether site distributions are accidental or the result of deliberate human action. They can also look at such questions as these: How was an area first settled? Why did sites split off one from another? What were the relationships between population density, settlement patterns, and the development of cities? But to approach these and many other related questions requires large quantities of raw data, a rarity in these days of expensive, small-scale excavations.

TRADE

Human subsistence is based on the exploitation of the natural environment. Many hunter-gatherer societies were self-sufficient in their dietary needs. They used only the raw materials within their regular territory. But many societies, especially after the invention of agriculture, were no longer self-sufficient. They needed access to a much wider range of raw materials and finished artifacts, many of which they obtained by trading with neighboring communities.

Much prehistoric trade took the form of simple exchange, often in the form of offering an object to a trading partner on the assumption that a return gift would be given in exchange at some future date. This form of trade is commonplace in New Guinea and the Pacific today. The bartering of day-to-day items like foodstuffs between villagers living in different environments was obviously conducted with one set of rules, while commodities accessible in commonly shared catchment zones, like obsidian (volcanic glass), were subject to quite different factors. Here, of course, the distance of a community from an obsidian source and the number of people requiring it may have set the pattern of exchange. Each community could, for example, barter communally for its raw materials, which might in turn be handed over to specialist craftspeople who produced the finished artifacts for others in the group.

Trade is normally recognized in the archaeological record by the discovery of exotic objects in sites miles away from their point of origin. The Indians of the Lake Superior region, for example, obtained copper from natural outcrops near the lake. They traded the precious metal over thousands of miles to as far away as Florida. Perhaps the most famous trade commodity of all is obsidian, widely prized for making knives and shiny mirrors. Obsidian is found at a few localities in the Near East and at many more in Mesoamerica. In the Near East, it has been possible to identify the sources of the obsidian found in early farming villages by comparing the trace elements in raw obsidian from the source areas with that in traded artifacts. After dozens of sites had been examined, Colin Renfrew and other archaeologists concluded that villages spaced at regular intervals were passing about half the obsidian they received to their more distant neighbors, so that small supplies were carried over enormous distances. In Mesoamerica, obsidian was traded in regional networks through informal trading relationships that gradually became more and more organized as new emerging local rulers began to control the valuable trade.

Trade, indeed, has been thought of as one variable that contributed to the origins of urban life and the increasing complexity of societies. Undoubtedly, trade became more complicated as social and political controls over raw materials and luxuries increased. This increased complexity may be reflected in the presence of a wider variety of exotic artifacts in individual sites.

But trade goods themselves are less important to archaeologists than the mechanisms that brought the goods to the site, so archaeologists have followed economists and geographers in looking at trading mechanisms. All prehistoric trade involved at least two parties. There is no such thing as trade in general. Each commodity creates specific problems of trading, particularly transportation problems. The motives for trading, too, are varied. People have traded for survival, for prestige, for religious reasons, and for wealth, to mention only a few reasons. In more complex societies, the ruler and his or her followers generally control trade. They develop and police trade networks and employ specialist merchants and traders to keep it going.

Take, for example, the lowland Maya of Mesoamerica. The Maya lived in a uniform, lowland rainforest environment that lacked rocks suitable for grinding maize, salt, obsidian, and many luxury materials. All these rocks could be obtained from the highlands and from the Valley of Mexico, as well as from Guatemala and elsewhere. But the necessary trading networks and connections to obtain these essentials had to be organized, not simply for individual communities but for the hundreds of lowland settlements with common assets, in an area where communications are very difficult. The Maya developed complex trade networks through the authority of the major ceremonial centers and their leaders. Imports like grinding stones and obsidian were exchanged down through the hierarchy of Maya settlements from the larger centers to smaller ones. These state-organized trade networks made the Maya communities very dependent on one another. As a result, a complex, widely distributed state society was developed.

These Maya trade networks are being studied through artifact patterns in hundreds of sites and the distribution of exotic tools and materials through the Maya lowlands. But these studies are only preliminary to considering trade as one of many elements in the prehistoric settlement pattern, one that served to link households, communities, and regions into trade networks controlled and regulated by chiefs, religious leaders, or specialist merchants. Many of these controls can be understood only if we examine prehistoric religious beliefs and social organization.

SOCIAL ORGANIZATION

Our old friend the cartoon archaeologist believed that you could never find out anything about peoples' social organization and religious beliefs from archaeological excavation. This is untrue. By studying artifact patterns and stylistic changes in material culture, one can gain some insights into prehistoric social organization.

Many anthropologists have defined several broad levels of sociocultural evolution in prehistory. These provide a general framework for tracing human social organization from the first simple family structures of the earliest humans to the highly complex state-organized societies of the early civilizations.

For most of prehistory, humanity flourished in **bands** of twenty-five to sixty people linked by kinship ties. This tightly knit organization encouraged cooperative hunting and gathering and sharing of resources. Then early farmers, with their more sedentary life, associated in groups of bands linked by kinship clans into **tribes.** All resources were owned by the tribe as a whole, and a tribal council would govern affairs. Among tribal societies where different kin groups assumed some order of rank, **chiefdoms** developed. The leaders of these lineages coordinated the management of food surplusses and the distribution of specialist products. Their authority was often maintained by their spiritual powers. **State-organized societies** developed out of chiefdoms. They were governed by a ruling class which headed a bureaucracy and governed through a justice system. The ownership of land and control of religion were in the leaders' hands. All society was ranked in social classes — warriors, traders, peasants, and so on. State-organized societies were the foundation of the earliest civilizations.

The archaeological evidence for social organization comes from several sources. Burials and their associated grave goods can give information on social ranking, information that can be obtained by studying the possessions and ornaments deposited with each skeleton in a site. A most spectacular example comes from the royal cemetery at Ur-of-the-Chaldees, Mesopotamia. The British archaeologist Leonard Woolley uncovered 1,850 graves, 16 of which stood out as special sepulchres because of their very rich grave furniture. The royal corpses were laid to rest in brick chambers accompanied by their personal attendants. The entire court and the royal bodyguard, complete with wagons and weapons, then lined up in order outside the burial chamber and lay down to die after taking poison. Woolley was able to describe the members of court, their order of precedence, and their distinctive costumes. All of these corpses contrasted sharply with the hundreds of humbler burials elsewhere in the cemetery.

Artifact Patterning and Settlement Patterns

When James Deetz studied the archaeology of the Arikara Indians of South Dakota, he used changes in pottery design as a means of examining alterations in social organization through time. He began by assuming that all the pots were made by women, and that mothers passed on styles to their daughters, as is often the case in Indian societies. He assumed also that there would be continuity in pottery designs through time, with each household perpetuating its pot styles over many generations. Deetz then excavated an Arikara site that was known to date to between A.D. 1700 and 1780. He found three occupation zones, each with distinctive pottery styles. The wares from the earliest levels fit into well-defined classes. Clearly, the designers had definite ideas about what each type of vessel should look like. But pottery in the two later occupations was much harder to classify, as if the closely knit cultural traditions of earlier generations had broken down. There were no tight clusterings of attributes to work with.

Deetz looked at contemporary historical records and found that the Arikara had moved up the Missouri more and more frequently between 1700 and 1800. A shortage of timber upstream caused them both to shift villages more often and to build smaller houses. When they moved into more open country, the men spent more and more time trading, acting as middlemen between white traders and Plains Indians. As farming became less important, female roles changed. Instead of living with their mothers, a situation that would lead to continuity in pottery styles, many women moved away to new villages. This was, Deetz concluded, reflected in more variable pottery traditions and other changes in artifact patterning.

The Deetz study is a fascinating experiment in using artifacts to study social structure, one of many such attempts in recent years. The Arikara conclusions have been challenged on several grounds. The site Deetz dug was occupied at a time when the Arikara were in contact with many groups and when population was falling sharply. Could the less-patterned styles reflect a period of depopulation — perhaps another explanation for the breakdown of family pottery styles? Much more fieldwork will be needed before Deetz's pioneer conclusions are confirmed.

Many archaeologists assume that there is a direct relationship between the degree to which people interacted with one another and the stylistic similarities of their pots and other artifacts. The problem is to test this assumption against the archaeological record. Unfortunately, there are few areas of the world with sufficient data to follow up on Deetz's pioneer attempt.

RELIGIOUS BELIEFS

An anonymous archaeologist once wrote cynically that "religion is the last resort of troubled archaeologists." At one time archaeologists tended to call any object they couldn't identify "ritual." Some still do. Obviously, some important

FIGURE 9.4   A Venus figurine head from Brassempouy, France. "The only way that we can hope to zero in on these types of fundamental beliefs is by looking at obvious religious artifacts and their patterning within archaeological sites."

sites were of religious significance. The Pyramid of the Sun at Teotihuacán is one, Stonehenge in England another. Some of the earliest religious objects in the world are the so-called Venus figurines made in Europe some twenty-five thousand years ago (Figure 9.4).

Some evidence for religious rituals comes from burials. The Neanderthal peoples of western Europe deliberately buried their dead seventy thousand years ago with a variety of goods. Hundreds of Adena and Hopewell burial mounds dot the landscape of the Midwest, containing the graves of thousands of clan leaders and lesser personages, each buried with distinctive grave furniture, some with elaborate cult objects. The building of the Hopewell mounds was carried out step by step, as the dead were deposited on an earthen platform that was later covered with a large mound. The famous Great Serpent Mound in Ohio is an example of a ceremonial earthwork whose exact religious significance still escapes us (Figure 9.5).

Many more-complex prehistoric societies enjoyed highly organized religions that were reflected in widely distributed and largely characteristic art styles. The Olmec art style of Mexico was carried over thousands of square miles of highlands and lowlands after 1000 B.C. Olmec art's snarling jaguar and human motifs coincide with a set of distinctive religious beliefs that linked large and small communities all over Mexico.

Most societies' religious beliefs were interpreted and maintained through regular religious rituals conducted at certain times of the year — such as at harvests and plantings. These regular ceremonies were vital to the elaborate organization of newly emerging complex societies. The predictable yearly round of religious life gave society an orderly framework for redistribution of food, disposing of surplus cattle, accumulation of wealth, and other economic functions. The long-term effects of these new, unifying religious beliefs were startling. Between 1150 and 850 B.C., for instance, Mesoamerican society began to undergo a rapid transformation. Administrative and religious authority came together in the hands of leaders of a newly ranked society, with specialists and a hierarchy of different settlements. This organization contrasted with the dispersed villages of earlier

FIGURE 9.5   The Great Serpent Mound, built by the Adena people as
a ceremonial earthwork.

times. More elaborate public buildings appear, as temples
and monumental buildings begin to reflect the common in-
volvement of individual communities in public works. In
Mesoamerica and elsewhere, there is a link between the ultimate sacred beliefs and rituals of a society and the processes
of social and environmental change that act upon it.

The only way that we can hope to zero in on these types of
fundamental beliefs is by looking at obvious religious artifacts and their patterning within archaeological sites. There
was, for example, a close relationship between the spread of
Mexican religious beliefs and the trading of fine art objects,
new pottery forms, conch shells, and the sting-ray spines
used in self-mutilation rites, as we know from painted mu-
rals. The distribution of such artifacts in areas away from the

Olmec lowlands, and the distribution of the same imports within individual villages, in houses and public buildings, can give us some clues as to when the new beliefs first took hold over a wider area. By studying burials and artifact patternings, as well as the artifacts themselves, we can gain insights into how religious beliefs acted as one of the many variables affecting the ever-changing societies of prehistoric times.

10

ARCHAEOLOGY TODAY AND TOMORROW

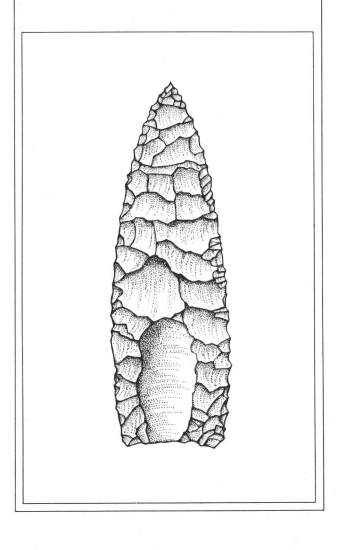

> The nation's past is contained in the soil. That
> soil is being distributed and redistributed at an ever
> increasing rate. Those of us alive today will be the
> last ever to see any significant portion of it in an
> undisturbed state.

CHARLES MCGIMSEY, 1973

THE LIVING PAST

We live in a world inhabited by an astonishing diversity
of human societies. A century ago, many of them were still
living in much the same way as their prehistoric ancestors.
But the unchanging routine of planting and harvest, of life
and death, of the seasons of game and vegetable foods has
withered in the face of Western exploration and technological superiority. Today, few of these societies are still enjoying their traditional lifeways. Many are extinct. The Tasmanians vanished within seventy years of white settlement; the
Indians of Tierra del Fuego in the 1950s (Figure 10.1). Ishi,
the last California hunter-gatherer, managed to live in his
home territory in the northern California foothills until 1911.
He saw all his companions wiped out by white settlers. The
surviving Indian peoples of the Amazon region are rapidly
fading away in the face of large-scale commercial operations
in their forest territories. Soon all traces of living prehistory
will be gone forever.

Anthropology has traditionally been concerned with non-
Western societies and with peoples who have had to make
far-reaching adjustments to the twentieth century. It is no
coincidence that anthropologists have followed these people

169

as they adjusted. Now anthropologists study their medical and psychological adjustments as the urban poor. But the archaeologist studies human culture of the past. Since 1877, many of the societies once studied by anthropologists have, by their death or transformation, become part of the archaeological record. No longer living groups, they have left behind them assemblages of artifacts, hierarchies of sites, a settlement pattern to be traced by surviving finds in the ground. The traditional cultures of the remaining hunter-gatherer and peasant societies are vanishing rapidly in the face of Western technology, plastics, chewing gum, and the transistor radio.

COMPARISONS

Early anthropologists collected vast quantities of information on traditional material culture of diverse societies all over the world. This material gave archaeologists a chance to make comparisons between still-living peoples and prehistoric peoples who lived at a similar stage of technological

FIGURE 10.1 A group of Fuegan Indians walking along the shore; these and many other hunter-gatherer peoples are now virtually extinct.

development. Thus, it was argued, the San, Australian aborigines, and other living hunter-gatherers who had no metals could be considered to be living representatives of prehistoric, stone-using hunter-gatherers. An archaeologist who dug a twenty-thousand-year-old camp site in an arctic environment, for instance, would turn to the Eskimo of today for comparative material from modern times.

But this type of comparison was obviously too simplistic. In the first place, human society did not necessarily pass through uniform stages of evolution (Chapter 1). Second, each society has its own distinctive adaptation to its environment, an adaptation which helps shape all aspects of its culture in many individual ways. And that adaptation was probably very different twenty thousand years ago.

Archaeologists then began to make analogies with recent societies in new ways. They worked back from known, living peoples into earlier times. They began by digging sites of historically documented Indians, and studying their contents, making full use of historical records to interpret their finds. Thus, photographs of Northwest Coast Indian homes taken in 1890 would be compared with excavated home foundations from comparatively recent times, say A.D. 1500. If the features of both were the same, then it was reasonable to interpret the design of prehistoric houses from this model. The house would then be traced backwards into prehistoric times in sites many centuries earlier than the historic settlements.

This, very simply stated, is the basis upon which archaeologists use ethnographic records to interpret prehistoric artifacts and sites. Considerable controversy surrounds such interpretations, for sophisticated research methods are needed if comparisons are to be made between modern artifact patternings and those found in prehistoric sites. It is for this reason that many archaeologists are developing a strong interest in "living" archaeology.

LIVING ARCHAEOLOGY

Much of the ethnographic data available to archaeologists was collected when anthropology was a much less sophisticated study than it is today. Very often ethnographers collected object after object or information on customs without recording detailed information on settlement layout or artifact patternings, the types of information that archaeologists now need so badly. One can hardly blame the pioneers, for they were concerned with recording as much information about vanishing cultures as they could before it was too late. And subtle settlement details hardly seemed a high priority.

Today, many of the settlements the anthropologists studied have become archaeological sites themselves. They are now virtually indistinguishable from prehistoric sites with their middens and crumbled hut foundations. They offer a unique opportunity to study the processes by which abandoned settlements turn into archaeological sites. An understanding of these processes makes archaeological interpretation in general much easier, so some archaeologists have gone out in the field to study "living archaeology" for themselves. Anthropologist Richard Lee, who has spent many years studying !Kung San of southern Africa, took archaeologist John Yellen with him on one of his later expeditions. Yellen spent many months studying the ways in which the San butchered animals and also the fragmentary bones that resulted from butchery, cooking, and eating (Figure 10.2). He drew plans of recently abandoned sites of known age, recorded the positions of houses, hearths, and occupation debris, and talked to people who had lived there, as a way of establishing precise population estimates and the social relationships of the inhabitants.

Yellen found that the San camps developed their layouts through conscious acts like building a shelter or a hearth as well as through such casual deeds as the discarding of animal bones and debris from toolmaking. There were communal areas that every one used and private family areas centered around hearths. Some activity areas, like places where women cracked nuts in the heat of the day, were simply located under a convenient, shady tree. Yellen recorded that most food preparation took place in family areas. Most activities in San camps were related to individual families. Theoretically, therefore, one should be able to study the development of the family through time by studying changing artifact patternings. To do so in practice, of course, requires very comprehensive data and carefully formulated research designs.

FIGURE 10.2 Living archaeology. A !Kung San brush shelter and windbreak, recorded by an archaeologist (F. Van Noten) shortly after it was abandoned. "Within a few generations, living archaeology will be a virtual impossibility."

Ethnography and archaeology can complement each other beautifully. When Richard Gould was looking for archaeological sites in the Australian western desert, he came across a few bands of nomadic aborigines. These local people not only guided him· to archaeological sites but also told him who had lived here, giving details of the sacred traditions associated with the settlements and describing the activities that had taken place at each one (Figure 10.3). At Puntutjarpa rockshelter, Gould excavated stone tools dating back from modern time to about 6,800 years ago. Many of them were indistinguishable from tools still used by the locals! The aborigines identified the tools for Gould, gave him their terminology, and explained how each one was used. Gould then studied ancient and modern tools, looked at the wear on the working surfaces, and was even able to say that some five-thousand-year-old stone tools had been hafted with wooden handles. He could make this statement with certainty because identical modern examples were so hafted. Gould's research was successful because he combined archaeology and ethnography to study not only individual artifacts but also patternings of artifacts in ancient and modern sites. He even used his modern data to estimate a prehistoric population density for the area of 3.55 persons per camp.

Living archaeology has the potential to produce important results, especially for settlement studies. But it is urgent research. The few surviving hunter-gatherers and farmers still enjoying their traditional culture are under constant threat of extinction. Within a few generations, living archaeology will be a virtual impossibility. Priceless information will be lost forever.

FIGURE 10.3 Comparison of a prehistoric campsite at Puntutjarpa rockshelter, Australia, at the right, with a modern Australian aborigine campsite.

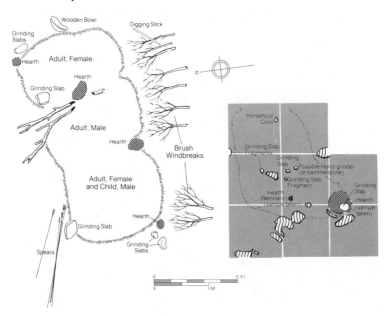

EXPERIMENTAL ARCHAEOLOGY

Archaeologists love experimenting with the past and have done so ever since the eighteenth century. One ardent early experimenter, a Dr. Robert Ball of Dublin, Ireland, blew a prehistoric horn so hard that he produced a sound like a bellowing bull. Unfortunately, his heroic efforts caused him to burst a blood vessel and die. Not all experimental archaeology is so risky, however. Archaeologists have been making stone implements, floating over oceans on rafts, and trying to recreate the past ever since. Some of their achievements are remarkable.

Louis Leakey not only dug prehistoric campsites, but also spent many years perfecting his skills as a stone toolmaker. He could shape a perfect prehistoric handaxe and skin an antelope with it in a few minutes — a favorite demonstration at a conference. One of the most remarkable experiments of all was Norwegian Thor Heyerdahl's *Kon-Tiki* expedition, on which he attempted to prove that Polynesia had been settled by adventurous Peruvians who had sailed balsa rafts across thousands of miles of ocean. Heyerdahl did succeed in reaching Polynesia. His expedition merely proved, however, that long ocean voyages in *Kon-Tiki* rafts were possible. He did not prove that the Peruvians settled Polynesia.

People have cleared thick Danish woodland with stone axes and grown prehistoric crops in the American Southwest under conditions identical to those of centuries ago. These latter experiments have lasted for seventeen years. Good crop yields were obtained in all but two years, when drought killed the young crops. Experiments at living the prehistoric life-style have proved popular, especially in Britain and Denmark, where television networks have financed long-term experiments involving volunteer "prehistoric peoples." Controlled burnings of some faithful reconstructions of ancient houses have been undertaken, too, to show what the structures would look like when reduced to ashes — as structures are in many actual sites. British archaeologists have even built an entire experimental earthwork which they are digging up at regular intervals over a period of 128 years. The resultant information on soil decay and artifact preservation will be invaluable for interpreting equivalent prehistoric sites.

Experimental archaeology is principally remembered for its spectacular tests, like *Kon-Tiki* or the blaring sound of Tutankhamun's trumpets, blown for the first time after 3,300 years. The amount of data that can be derived from controlled experiments is, however, limited. Many intangible variables affected the design and use of prehistoric artifacts. And, as always, very precise research designs and carefully controlled data are needed to take proper account of such intangibles.

THE FUTURE OF THE PAST

Experimental and living archaeology bring us into intimate association with the present, with the archaeologist as anthropologist. No one confronted with the results of Gould's work in Australia or the many excavations on Indian pueblos in the Southwest can doubt the essential continuity between many of the world's recent societies and the long millennia of prehistoric times. Anthropology tells a story of human biological and cultural evolution that climaxes in the emergence of urban civilization and the extraordinary diversity of the modern world. But the very emergence of civilization has hastened the evolution of new, much larger, global societies. Scores of societies are now linked by common religious beliefs, political ideologies, or remarkable heights of technological achievement. Our own Western society with its abilities at instant communication and its capacity to feed more people than ever before has reached out to the farthest corners of the world in search of new economic and spiritual domains to conquer. The results for many societies have been traumatic.

The Polynesians encountered the Western world in the eighteenth century. A hundred years later, they were a shadow of their previous selves, exploited and missionized almost to death. Millions of American Indians perished as the frontier of the United States pushed inexorably westward. Few bands of Australian aborigines retain even a part of their millennia-old culture. The alternatives for the members of these societies were extinction or assimilation into a culture where they were, at best, second-rate citizens. It is only in the 1960s and 1970s that some of them have been able to stand on their own feet again, as newly independent groups or nations trying to reestablish their identity in a much-changed world.

The emergence of nationalism can be seen as one of the major historical trends of recent decades. It is manifested in new nations and in ethnic minorities who have begun an ardent search for their own historical identity. Alex Haley's *Roots* rightly caused a sensation when it recounted how Haley found his ancestry in West Africa. For many people, such oral traditions were lost in the enormous adjustment their nonliterate societies have made in the past century. Thus, archaeology remains the primary source of historical data about the Australian aborigines, the Tahitians, the American Indians and hundreds of other non-Western societies. If anyone asks whether archaeology has any use, one has only to point to the huge gaps in world history that still await the archaeologists' attention — if there are any sites left to excavate.

The breathtaking pace of agricultural and industrial development in recent years has taken a massive toll of the past. Thousands of American Indian sites have been destroyed by flooding under hydroelectric dams, deep plowing and strip mining, and thousands of acres of new urban development and freeway construction. Pot hunters, too, have taken their toll. We may be the last generation of Americans to see many undisturbed archaeological sites. Charles McGimsey of the University of Arkansas has estimated that few untouched sites remain in his state. There are probably less than five percent undisturbed sites left in Los Angeles County. Despite a series of new antiquities laws in recent years, which mainly protect sites on federal land, there is a real danger that archaeology in North America is doomed. The finite resource base of sites is being eroded with an unthinking lack of concern for the history these priceless archives contain. It is genocide, not of the living, but of the dead.

The popular interest in archaeology still revolves around ancient mysteries, the excitement of discovery — and buried treasure. Many people regard archaeology as a luxury with no relevance to the cultural history of humankind. It is a means of gratifying their urge to possess things. Projectile points, Maya pots, and bronze swords look good on a mantle shelf or in a museum display case. So great is the demand for such treasures that a flourishing antiquities market has grown up to satisfy our greedy urges. Archaeological sites have been destroyed for commercial ends ever since the eighteenth century. The early collections of the Metropolitan Museum of Art in New York and many other major museums were very often accumulated by purchase of looted objects handled by large-scale dealers in the past. Today's prices are astronomical. So much damage has been done that more and more museums and wealthy collectors are competing for fewer and fewer finds. Entire Inca cemeteries and Maya ceremonial centers have been decimated in search of saleable objects. Many sites in the American Southwest had been ravaged beyond repair by the early years of this century.

Almost nothing can be, or has been, done about the illegal trade in antiquities. Unscrupulous collectors and museums do not care, the dealers do not care, and the treasure hunting supports whole villages of poor farmers in Costa Rica and other countries. Worst of all, the public as a whole does not care. Unfortunately, the future of archaeology lies in everyone's hands, and many people destroy archaeological sites without realizing it or because they consider them useless (Figure 10.4).

ARCHAEOLOGY AND YOU

How can you become involved in archaeology? Are there career prospects as an archaeologist? What can a lay person do to help save the past? There are many ways to become involved.

Hundreds of archaeologists work in the United States. Many teach in universities and colleges, some in high schools. Others head up archaeological departments of national, city, state, or local museums all over the country or direct state archaeological surveys. Archaeologists work for the National Park Service and other federal agencies. Others support themselves by part-time teaching or undertake contracts on federal projects or for companies seeking cultural resource management services.

The research interests of these archaeologists range from early Indian settlements on the plains to historical sites in New England, from theoretical models of early agriculture to

FIGURE 10.4 Two possibilities for the future of the past. At the top, removal of the Abu Simbel temples was an international effort at rescue archaeology. Here, the face of Ramesses II is lifted to the new location of the Great Temple. At the bottom, pot hunters at work do irreparable damage to a site. Compare this scene of devastation with the excavations illustration in Chapter 6.

computer simulation. There are almost more specialities than archaeologists. And a considerable number of America's archaeologists work overseas — in Africa, Europe, Mesoamerica, Peru, and even farther afield. You can find someone who will teach you almost any type of archaeology you want, above or below ground, under the water, even in the air! Unfortunately, however, job opportunities are in short supply.

Most archaeological jobs, whether in a college, museum, or university require a minimum of a master's degree, most often the doctorate as well. The doctorate is a research degree requiring comprehensive seminar, course, and field training in graduate school and then a period of intensive fieldwork that, when written up, forms the dissertation, which is submitted to a committee of examiners. The average doctoral program takes between four and seven years to complete. Once you have the degree, you still have to find a job as a faculty member or museum officer somewhere. And that, in these days of great numbers of Ph.D.'s, is not easy.

The M.A. degree normally takes one or two years of graduate work and gives you a broad, general training in the basic methods and theory of archaeology, as well as world prehistory, with some specialization in a local area or in cultural resource management. The degree is satisfied by courses and seminars. You may have to write a library thesis as well and obtain some digging experience. The M.A. can qualify you to teach at two-year colleges and some state universities. Although it does not give you as much access to research funds and opportunities as a Ph.D., you can do invaluable work in cultural resource management or local archaeology. Various universities and colleges do offer certification programs for people interested in contract, conservation archaeology, work for which no Ph.D. and sometimes not even an M.A. is required. Consult your professors about these opportunities.

Anyone considering becoming a professional archaeologist must have a superior academic record with an in-depth coverage of anthropology and archaeology. A grade point average of "A" is a minimal requirement for good graduate schools. Some field experience on a dig or survey is also necessary, as is strong and meaningful support from at least two qualified archaeologists able to write letters for you. As for attitude, a strong motivation to become an archaeologist is a must, and, for the Ph.D., a specific research interest. An archaeologist who thrives on hard work and who can tolerate some discomfort, a mass of detail, and long hours of routine laboratory work will be a happy one. And those interested in the field should also be able to face up to a very tight employment situation. An interest in teaching and a moral commitment not to collect artifacts for profit or personal gain are the remaining prerequisites in this formidable list. If the list sounds severe, remember that archaeologists of the next generation have the future of the past in their hands.

Let's say you do want to become an archaeologist. Which graduate school should you apply to? This depends on your specific interests, and you should choose your school accordingly. It is wise to apply to more than one department and to make sure first that your faculty advisers really support your application.

Many people want to gain some digging experience whether they intend to go to graduate school or not. The best way to learn is to take a course in field methods, then volunteer to dig for a period on a summer excavation. Details of digs are normally posted on anthropology department bulletin boards or at local museums. Some people elect to go on a university-sponsored field school and to obtain academic credit for their work. Many such schools are designed mainly for graduate students, but, again, you should consult your own department. General field schools, like the Koster dig in Illinois, are worthwhile because they combine excavation, laboratory analysis, and academic instruction in one intensive experience. And the camaraderie of such digs can be a memorable experience.

Some people venture farther afield and join an excavation overseas for some weeks. Cheap charter flights have made Europe readily accessible. By contacting such organizations as the Council for British Archaeology in London, it is possible to obtain details of excavations in progress where volunteers are needed. Bear in mind that very few digs, in this country or overseas, pay you to be an excavator. At the costly end of the spectrum are package travel tours that take students to such faraway places as Israel to dig and learn archaeology under close supervision. These tend to be expensive experiences, often of variable academic quality. But whatever type of dig you choose, an excavation experience is a good way of testing out your commitment to archaeology.

An undergraduate degree in archaeology is insufficient qualification for a job in the subject. But good undergraduate training can give you a perspective on archaeology that will be with you for the rest of your life. There are many ways to enjoy archaeology as an interested lay person. You can join a local archaeological society, participate in excavations and volunteer museum programs, keep an eye on endangered sites in your community. The background in archaeology you take with you into later life will enable you to visit famous sites all over the world as an informed visitor, to enjoy the achievements of prehistoric peoples to the full. Above all, you can influence the way other people think about, and behave toward, archaeological sites and accidental discoveries. And your contacts with former instructors and other professional archaeologists may help you prevent damage to important, undisturbed sites.

This book may be the only experience many of you have of archaeology. We hope it has given you some insight into how archaeologists reconstruct the prehistoric past. But how can you help save the past for future generations? How should responsible people live with the finite resources of prehistory? Here are some fundamental guidelines:

Treat every archaeological site and artifact as a finite resource that can never be replaced once destroyed.

Report all archaeological discoveries to responsible archaeological authorities (archaeological surveys, museums, university or college departments, government agencies).

Obey all laws relating to archaeological sites.

Never dig a site without proper training or supervision.

Never collect archaeological finds from any country for your private collection or for profit. If you must collect, collect reproductions.

Respect modern and prehistoric Indian burial grounds and sacred sites. They have deep spiritual significance to their owners.

Is there a future for the past? Yes, if we want there to be. It is up to all of us.

FURTHER READING

The technical literature of archaeology is so immense that we cannot guide you to more than a few key references on each of the major topics covered in this book. For more detailed information, consult one of the major summaries listed here or ask your instructor.

General Summaries

Two major college texts provide a comprehensive background to the method and theory of prehistoric archaeology. This text is a much-shortened version of my own *In the Beginning* (Little, Brown: Boston, 4th ed., 1981). R. J. Sharer and Wendy Ashmore, *Fundamentals of Archaeology* (Benjamin/Cummings: Menlo Park, 1980) is an equivalent volume.

The major events of world prehistory are described in Grahame Clark, *World Prehistory in New Perspective* (Cambridge University Press: Cambridge, 3rd ed., 1977) and in my *People of the Earth* (Little, Brown: Boston, 4th ed., 1983). Another excellent account: Robert Wenke, *Patterns in Prehistory* (Oxford University Press: New York, 1979).

cc 75.547

Special Fields of Archaeology

Historical Archaeology: Ivor Nöel Hume, *Historical Archaeology* (Alfred Knopf: New York, 1968). Classical archaeology is summarized by Paul L. McKendrick, *The Greek Stones Speak* and *The Mute Stones Speak* (both St. Martin's Press: New York, 1962 and 1961). Underwater archaeology is covered by George Bass, *Archaeology Underwater* (Praeger: New York, 1966) and the same author's magnificent *A History of Seafaring Based on Underwater Archaeology* (Thames and Hudson: London, 1972).

Atlases and Dictionaries of Archaeology

The best atlas for the general student is David and Ruth Whitehouse, *Archaeological Atlas of the World* (W. H. Freeman: San Francisco, 1975). A good dictionary: Warwick Bray and David Trump, *A Dictionary of Archaeology* (Penguin Press: London, 1970).

Major Archaeological Journals

There are dozens of international, national, and local archaeological journals, designed mainly for specialists. Among those carrying popular articles of archaeology are *Early Man, National Geographic, Nature, Natural History, Scientific American,* and *Smithsonian. Archaeology* is widely read by interested lay people, while *Antiquity* and *World Archaeology* are truly international journals that carry articles of wide interest to all archaeologists. American archaeologists rely heavily on *American Antiquity,* the journal of the Society for American Archaeology. *American Anthropologist* sometimes carries archaeological pieces, while Old World archaeologists publish in *Man, Nature,* and the *Proceedings of the Prehistoric Society.* The *Journal of field Archaeology* is of high technical value.

Chapter 1:   Archaeology as Anthropology

James Deetz, *Invitation to Archaeology* (Natural History Press: Garden City, New York, 1967), covers many of the points in this chapter. So does Grahame Clark, *Archaeology and Society* (Barnes and Noble: New York, 1965) — an old account which has never been bettered. Rose Macaulay, *The Pleasure of Ruins* (Thames and Hudson: London, 1959) is a delight for tourists. Massimo Pallotino, *The Meaning of Archaeology* (Abrams: New York, 1968) is a thoughtful account of the issues raised in this chapter. A history of archaeology: Glyn Daniel, *A Short History of Archaeology* (Thames and Hudson: London, 1981). For American archaeology: Gordon Willey and Jeremy Sabloff, *A History of American Archaeology* (W. H. Freeman: San Francisco, 1974).

Chapter 2: Culture and the Archaeological Record

Few archaeologists have dared to write a summary of the controversial issues covered in this chapter. Gordon Willey and Philip Phillips, *Method and Theory in American Archaeology* (University of Chicago Press: Chicago, 1958) is fundamental. So is V. Gordon Childe's insightful *Piecing Together the Past* (Routledge and Kegan Paul: London, 1956). Later developments in archaeology can be surveyed in Lewis and Sally Binford, eds., *New Perspectives in Archaeology* (Aldine: Chicago, 1968) and in Lewis Binford, *An Archaeological Perspective* (Seminar Press: New York, 1972). See also P. J. Watson, C. L. Redman, and S. LeBlanc, *Explanation in Archaeology* (Free Press: New York, 1973). Charles Redman, ed., *Research and Theory in Current Archaeology* (Wiley Interscience: New York, 1973) contains valuable critiques of recent developments in the field. Michael Jochim, *Strategies for Survival* (Academic Press: New York, 1981) is vital on ecology.

Chapter 3: Time

Two key references: J. W. Michels, *Dating Methods in Archaeology* (Seminar Press: New York, 1973) and H. N. Michael and E. K. Ralph, eds., *Dating Techniques for the Archaeologist* (MIT Press: Cambridge, 1971). Karl Butzer, *Environment and Archaeology* (Aldine: Chicago, 2nd ed., 1964) is fundamental for the Pleistocene. No one has yet rivaled Sir Mortimer Wheeler's classic description of stratigraphy in his *Archaeology from the Earth* (Clarendon Press: Oxford, 1954).

Chapter 4: Space

Once again, V. Gordon Childe, *Piecing Together the Past* (Routledge and Kegan Paul: London, 1956) is one of the few accounts. Kent V. Flannery, ed., *The Early Mesoamerican Village* (Academic Press: New York, 1976) covers some key concepts, but is better read in the context of Chapter 9. For the law of association, read John Rowe's paper: "Worsaae's Law and the Use of Grave Lots for Archaeological Dating," *American Antiquity* (1962), 28: 2, 129–137.

Chapter 5:   Preservation and Survey

There is no comprehensive treatment of preservation in archaeological sites. Here are some examples of outstanding
sites: John Romer, *The Valley of Kings* (William Morrow: New
York, 1981) is fascinating on Ancient Egyptian tombs, including Tutankhamun. The Koster site in Illinois: Stuart Streuver
and Gail Houart, *Koster* (Anchor Doubleday: New York, 1980).
P. V. Glob, *The Bog People* (Faber and Faber: London, 1969)
describes a series of well-preserved prehistoric corpses from
waterlogged Danish bogs. Even the skin and intestines survive. Sergei I. Rudenko, *Frozen Tombs of Siberia: The Pazyryk
Burials of Iron Age Horsemen* (University of California Press:
Berkeley, 1970), as translated by M. W. Thompson, examines
spectacular prehistoric graves where the permafrost soil has
literally refrigerated such organic materials as rugs. The
remarkable Ozette site is described by Ruth Kirk, with
Richard Daugherty in *Hunters of the Whale* (Morrow: New
York, 1975). Archaeological survey has been poorly served as
well, while references on cultural resource management and
antiquities legislation are far from accessible to the general
reader. Try Charles McGimsey, *Public Archaeology* (Seminar
Press: New York, 1972) and T. F. King, Patricia P. Hickman,
and Gary Berg, eds., *Anthropology in Historic Preservation: Car-
ing for Culture's Clutter* (Academic Press: New York, 1978).
George Gumerman and Michael Schiffer, eds., *Conservation
Archaeology* (Academic Press: New York, 1978) also contains
useful material.

Chapter 6:   Excavation

The most widely available manual of excavation methods is
Robert Heizer and J. Graham, *A Guide to Archaeological Field
Methods* (National Press: Palo Alto, 3rd ed., 1966). Mortimer
Wheeler, *Archaeology from the Earth* (Clarendon Press: Ox-
ford, 1954) is an immortal account of the basic principles,
based on large sites. Phillip Barker, *The Techniques of Ar-
chaeological Excavation* (Batsford: London, 1977) and Martha
Joukowsky, *A Complete Manual of Field Archaeology* (Prentice
Hall: Englewood Cliffs, N.J., 1981) are basic sources for the

serious student. For sampling: John A. Mueller, ed., *Sampling in Archaeology* (University of Arizona Press: Tucson, 1974).

Chapter 7:   Ordering the Past

V. Gordon Childe, *Piecing Together the Past* (Routledge and Kegan Paul: London, 1956) is still one of the best accounts of the problems of ordering. So is Gordon Willey and Philip Phillips, *Method and Theory in American Archaeology* (University of Chicago Press: Chicago, 1958), which describes some of the archaeological units used in the New World. Robert Dunnell's *Systematics in Prehistory* (Free Press: New York, 1970) is a technical but fascinating account of classification problems. The concept of type is covered in this book, while the article by Albert Spaulding referred to by the director is "Statistical Techniques for the Study of Artifact Types," *American Antiquity* (1953), 18: 4, 305–313. Cultural process: Bruce Trigger, *Beyond History: The Methods of Prehistory* (Holt, Rinehart and Winston: New York, 1968). See also Fred Plog, *The Study of Prehistoric Change* (Academic Press: New York, 1974) and Michael Schiffer, *Behavioral Archaeology* (Academic Press: New York, 1976). Patty Jo Watson, Steven A. LeBlanc, and Charles Redman, *Explanation in Archaeology* (Columbia University Press: New York, 1971) is a clear exposition of new approaches to the study of cultural process. No serious student should miss Kent Flannery, "The Cultural Evolution of Civilizations," *Annual Review of Ecology and Systematics* (1972), pp. 399–436.

Chapter 8:   Subsistence

We badly need a definitive work on prehistoric subsistence and the reconstruction of early diet. Anyone interested in this fascinating topic has to go through a series of books on different aspects of the subject. These include R. E. Chaplin, *The Study of Animal Bones in Archaeological Sites* (Seminar Press: New York, 1971). Lewis Binford's *Bones* (Academic Press: New York, 1981) discusses the basic issues of animal bone identification, analysis, and preservation. For plants: Jane

Renfrew, *Palaeoethnobotany* (Methuen: London, 1973). The Tehuacán discoveries are summarized by Richard MacNeish, *The Prehistory of the Tehuacán Valley* (University of Texas Press: Austin, Vol. 1, 1967), while Frank Hole, Kent V. Flannery, and A. J. Neely, *Prehistory and Human Ecology of the Deh Luran Plain* (Anthropology Museum of University of Michigan: Ann Arbor, 1969) describes the Deh Luran finds. Peter J. Ucko and G. W. Dimbleby, eds., *The Domestication and Exploitation of Plant and Animals* (Aldine: Chicago, 1969) contains many useful essays.

Chapter 9:   Interaction

K. C. Chang, *Settlement Archaeology* (National Press: Palo Alto, 1968) is a basic source, while Kent V. Flannery, ed., *The Early Mesoamerican Village* (Academic Press: New York, 1976) is essential reading for everyone interested in this subject, if only for the fascinating and hypothetical dialogues which communicate different viewpoints about contemporary archaeology. Teotihuacán: René Millon and others, *Urbanization at Teotihuacán, Mexico* (University of Texas Press: Austin, Vol. 1, 1973). A recent superb monograph on settlement archaeology: W. T. Sanders, Jeffrey R. Parsons, and Robert S. Santley, *The Basin of Mexico: Ecological Processes in the Evolution of a Civilization* (Academic Press: New York, 1979).

For social organization, see James Deetz, "The Dynamics of Stylistic Change in Arikara Ceramics," *Illinois Studies in Archaeology* (1965), No. 4. Olmec: Ignatio Bernal, *The Olmec World* (University of California Press: Berkeley, 1969). Ur-of-the-Chaldees: Leonard Woolley, *Excavations at Ur* (Charles Scribner Sons: New York, 1954) is a popular account.

Chapter 10:   Archaeology Today and Tomorrow

The literature is astonishingly sparse on the topics covered by this chapter. For living archaeology, see Richard Gould, *Living Archaeology* (Cambridge University Press: Cambridge, 1980). The !Kung San: Richard B. Lee, *The !Kung San* (Cambridge University Press: Cambridge, 1979). This book provides background on all aspects of !Kung life-style referred to in these pages. John Coles, *Archaeology by Experiment* (Hutch-inson University Press: London, 1973) is the best summary of this subject. Karl Meyer, *The Plundered Past* (Atheneum Press: New York, 1973) is required reading for all archaeol-ogists and nonarchaeologists. Charles McGimsey, *Public Archaeology* (Seminar Press: New York, 1972) highlights the crisis in archaeology.

(Englewood Cliffs, N.J.: Prentice-Hall, Inc., 1966), by permission of the publisher and author; Figure 7.4: From *Invitation to Archaeology* by James Deetz. Copyright © 1967 by James Deetz. Redrawn by permission of Doubleday & Company, Inc.

Figure 8.1: After Sonia Cole, *The Neolithic Revolution*, London 1959. By permission of the Trustees of the British Museum (Natural History); Figure 8.2b: Redrawn from M. L. Ryder, *Animal Bones in Archaeology* (Oxford: Blackwell Scientific Publications Ltd., 1969); Figure 8.3: Cambridge University Museum of Archaeology and Anthropology; Figure 8.4: Patricia Vinnecombe, "A Fishing Scene from the Tsoelike River, South-Eastern Basutoland," *South African Archaeological Bulletin* 15:57, March 1960, p. 15.

Figure 9.1: From *Urbanization at Teotihuacán, Mexico*, vol. 1, part 1, © 1973 by René Millon, by permission of the author; Figures 9.2a and 9.2b: Redrawn from *The Early Mesoamerican Village*, edited by Kent V. Flannery (New York: Academic Press, 1976), figs. 4.6 and 4.7; Figure 9.4: Musée de l'Homme, Paris; Figure 9.5: Courtesy of Museum of the American Indian, Heye Foundation, N.Y.

Figure 10.1: Colonel Charles Wellington Furlong; Figure 10.2: Dr. F. L. Van Noten, Musée Royal de l'Afrique Centrale; Figure 10.3: Redrawn from Richard A. Gould, "The Archaeologist as Ethnographer," *World Archaeology* 3:2, 1971, pp. 143–177, fig. 10; Figure 10.4: UNESCO; Figure 10.5: Hester A. Davis, from "Is There a Future for the Past?" *Archaeology* 24:4, © 1971, Archaeological Institute of America.

INDEX

Aborigines, 12
  in Tasmania, 14
Abri Pataud rockshelter, 103
Abu Simbel temples, 179
Accidental discoveries,
      86–88
Acheulian stone axes, 73
  and culture, 123
Activity areas, 66–67
  illustration, 68
Adena Indians
  bural of, 109
  inevitable variation
      among, 125–126
  religious beliefs, 165
Aerial photography, 82–84
Aging meat, 137–139
Agriculture
  analyzing remains of,
      139–142
  development of, 127
  origins of, 13
Ainu, 12
Ali Kosh mound, 141
Analytical types, 118–119
Animal bones, 134–139
Anthropology, 16–19
  goals of, 19–22
Apple Creek site, 141
Archaeological culture. See
      Culture
Archaeological record, 30–33
Archaeological sites. See
      Sites
Archaeological surveys. See
      Surveys
Area excavation, 97–98
Arikara Indians, 162–163
Arnold, J. R., 54, 55
Art sites, 33

Chavín art style, 123, 124,
      128
  Olmec art style, 165
  rock art, 145–146
Artifacts, 32, 33–36
  associations, see
      Association, law of
  attributes, see Attributes
  clusters, 119–120
  patterning, 162–164
  preservation, 72–78
  and relative chronology,
      41–45
Assemblages, 63, 65–66, 120
Association, law of, 61–63
  illustration of, 64
Attributes, 35–36
  clusters, 119–120
  and context, 36–37
  defined, 115
Automobile design changes,
      28–29
Aztec civilization, 11
  Teotihuacán, see
      Teotihuacán Valley

Bacon, Francis, 72
Ball, Robert, 175
Bandelier, Adolph, 17, 18
Bands, 161–162
Barbarism stage, 12
Battleship curve, 44–45
Bering Strait, 12
Binford, Lewis, 21–22
Bird bones, 142
Boas, Franz, 16
Brown, James, 92–93
Buildings, 149–150
Burial house, diagram of, 28

Burial sites
  excavation of, 107–110
  finding, 78
  Incas, 30
  and law of association, 63
  Leubingen, East Germany,
    28
  preservation of, 72–78
  and religious beliefs,
    164–167
  seriation of gravestones,
    43, 45
  Tutankhamun, *see*
    Tutankhamun
  Ur-of-the-Chaldees, *see*
    Ur-of-the-Chaldees
Butchering practices,
  137–139

C14 dating. *See* Radiocarbon
    dating
Calendar, Mayan, 40
Carbon isotope dating. *See*
    Radiocarbon dating
Catchment area, 153–156
Catherwood, Frederick, 80
Caves, excavation of, 103
Cemeteries. *See* Burial sites
Central place theory, 158–159
Century Ranch site, 143
Ceremonial sites. *See*
    Religious sites
Chart of prehistory events, 15
Chavín art style, 123, 124
  diffusion of, 128
Chiefdoms, 162
Childe, V. Gordon, 24
Christaller, Walter, 158–159
Chronology. *See* Relative
    chronology
Chronometric dating, 51–58
  fission track dating, 57
  major methods, chart of, 52
  potassium argon dating,
    57–58
  radiocarbon dating, *see*
    Radiocarbon dating
  tree-ring dating, *see*
    Tree-ring dating

Chumash Indians, 143
Civilization stage, 12
Classical archaeologists, 8
Classification, 113–120
  type description for, 117
Clusters of attributes,
    119–120
Coins and cross dating, 45
Communities, 66–67
  illustration, 68
  interaction of, 151–153
  as unit of order, 121
Components, 121
Computers for data, 21
Conservation archaeology, 81
Contexts, 7, 36–37
  space, *see* Space
Convenience typing,
    118–119
Copán, 33
Coprolites, 134
Cortés, Hernando, 11, 86
Coxcatlán Cave, 96
Cretans, 14
  trade among, 51
Cross dating, 45
Cultural ecology, 129–130
Cultural process, 27–30,
    125–130
Cultural resource
    management, 81
Cultural selection, 126
Cultural systems, 26–27
Culture, 24–30
  area, 67–68
  history, 20
  and phase, 121, 123
  process, 27–30, 125–130
  systems, 26–27
Cushing, Frank Hamilton, 17

Danger Caves, 103
Darwin, Charles, 11
Dating
  chronometric, *see*
    Chronometric dating
  cross dating, 45
Daugherty, Richard, 74, 77,
    94, 100

Death Valley, California, 32
Deetz, James, 2, 45, 162–163
Dendrochronology. *See*
        Tree-ring dating
Dethlefsen, Edwin, 45
Diet, 131–146
Diffusion, 127–128
Digs. *See* Excavations
Diospolis Parva, Egypt, 43
Distributions among sites,
        156
Domestic animals, 136–137
Dordogne Valley caves, 103

Earthworks, excavation of,
        105
Ecology, cultural, 129–130
Egypt
    early civilization, 13
    trade in, 51–52
Environments, study of,
        20–21
Eskimos, preservation of
        sites, 76
Ethnographers, 16
Euphrates river, 13
Evans, Arthur, 51–52
Excavations, 32, 89–110
    of burial sites, 107–110
    of habitation sites,
            101–106
    methods for, 98–100
    personnel for, 98, 100
    recordkeeping, 100–101
    research design, 91–93
    tools for, 100
    types of, 96–98
    Williamsburg, Virginia,
            8–9
Experimental archaeology,
        175–176
Explanatory ordering,
        124–125
Extinct peoples, 169

Farming. *See* Agriculture
Feces, 134
Fish remains, 143–144

Fission track dating, 57
Flannery, Kent, 130, 141, 150,
        153, 156
Flooded sites, 74
Flotation methods, 140–141
Food, 131–146
    study of remains, 20
Forts, excavation of, 105
Frozen sites, 76
Functional types, 116, 118

Galatea Bay, New Zealand,
        107
Game animals, 135–136
Garden of Eden, 11
Gizeh pyramids, 3, 13, 30
    excavation of, 107
    preservation of, 77
Goals of anthropology, 19–22
Gould, Richard, 173–174, 176
Grain impressions, 140
Graves. *See* Burial sites
Gravestones, seriation, 43, 45
Great Plains, 12
Great Serpent Mound, 165,
        166
Guattan Tomb, Guatemala,
        108
Guidelines for
        archaeologists, 182

Habitation sites, 33
    excavation of, 101–106
Hadar, Ethiopia, 58
Haley, Alex, 177
Hay Hollow Valley, 80
Heizer, Robert, 60
Heyerdahl, Thor, 175
Hierarchies of sites, 157–159
Historical archaeologists, 8
Hogup Caves, 103
    occupation of, 121
Hole, Frank, 141
Hopewell Indians
    burial of, 109
    earthworks of, 105
    inevitable variation
            among, 125–126
    religious beliefs, 165

Hopi Indians, 128
House designs, 150
Households, 66–67
    illustration, 68
Howard, Hildegarde, 142
Human prehistory, 11
Hunter-gatherer camps,
        excavation of, 101–103
Huxley, Thomas, 11

Ice Age, relative chronology,
        47–51
Inca cemeteries, 30
Indus River, 14
Inevitable variations,
        125–126
Interactions, 147–167
Invention, 126–127
Ipiutak culture, 78
Ironmaking, 126
Iroquois long house, 97
Ishi, 169
Iversen, Johannes, 141–142

Jobs for archaeologists,
        180–182

K atoms, dating by, 57–58
Kalahari desert. See
        !Kung San
Karnak, Egypt, Temple of
        Amun, 33
Kidder, A. V., 17, 18
Kill sites, 33
    animal bones from, 135
    identification of, 66
Kon-Tiki expedition, 175
Koobi Fora, Kenya, 58
Koster site, 92
!Kung San, 25
    analysis of, 172–173
    eating taboos of, 136
    seeds and roots of, 142
    settlement pattern of,
        69–70

Lake Superior Indians, 159
Lake Turkana, Kenya, 58
Lakes of Pleistocene, 47, 50

Larger scale ordering units,
        123
Law of association. See
        Association, law of
Leakey, Louis, 101, 139, 175
Leakey, Mary, 101, 102
Lee, Richard, 172
Lehmer, D. J., 116–117
Leubingen, East Germany
        burial house, 28
Libby, W. F., 54, 55
Living archaeology, 168–182
Livingstone, David, 144
Local sequence, 121
Lovelock Cave, 134
Lucretius, 148

MacNeish, Richard, 141
M.A. degrees, 180
Magnetic detecting, 86
Maiden Castle, England, 105
Makah Indians, 74, 76, 77, 94
Malinowski, Bronislaw, 16
Maoris
    culture area, 68
    earthworks, 105
Map of sites, 4–6
Martin, Paul, 80
Mayans
    burial sites, 108, 109
    calendar of, 40
    religious sites, 33
    remote sensing for sites,
        84–85
    settlement patterns, 70
    surveys for sites, 80
    trade among, 160–161
McGimsey, Charles, 169, 177
Mesa Verde, 53
Mesopotamians
    city mounds, 32
    delta, 13
Metropolitan Museum of
        Art, 7, 178
Mexico City, 86–87
Migration, 128–129
Millon, René, 106, 129,
        151–152
Mine detectors, 86

Minoan civilization, 51–52
Missing link, 11
Modern households, 10
Mollusk remains, 144
Mounds, excavation of, 104–105
Movius, Hallam, 103
Mudslides, preservation in, 74, 76
Museums at sites, 7
Mycenaeans, 14

Natural types, 116, 118
Neanderthal peoples
  burial sites, 107
  religious beliefs, 165
Nile Valley preservation, 74
Northwest Coast Indians, 143, 171

Oaxacan Valley, 129
  catchment areas, 153–156
  structures in, 150
Obsidian, 159, 160
Ohio earthworks, 30
Olduvai Gorge, 30, 32, 33
  discovery of, 97
  excavation of, 101–103
  occupation of, 39
Olmec art style, 165
Olsen-Chubbuck site, 139
Ordering, 111–130
  units of, 120–125
Ozette village, 74, 76, 77, 94

Pakistan, Indus River, 14
Palenque, 80
Palynology, 50
Patagonia, 12
Patterning, 26, 27
Patterns
  for attribute clusters, 120
  settlement, 68–70
Pazyryk burial mounds, 76
Pecos Pueblo, 17
Petrie, Flinders, 41, 44, 45
Phase, 121
Ph.D. degrees, 180–181
Photography, aerial, 82–84

Physical anthropology, 16
Piggott, Stuart, 2
Plant remains, 139–142
Pleistocene, relative
    chronology, 47–51
Plog, Fred, 80
Pollen samples, 50
Polynesia
  Kon-Tiki expedition, 175
  migration in, 128
  Tahitians, 16
Pope, Alexander, 112
Potassium argon dating, 57–58
Prehistoric archaeologists, 10
Prehistory, 8, 11–16
  chart of major events, 15
Preservation, 72–78
Probabilistic sampling, 94–96
Process, cultural, 27–30, 125–130
Proton magnetometer, 86
Pueblo Bonito site, 18
  and tree-ring dating, 53
Pueblo Indians, 12
  and Bandelier, Adolph, 16
  and tree-ring dating, 53
Puntutjarpa rockshelter, 173–174

Quarry sites, 33

Radar sensors, 84–86
Radiocarbon dating, 54–57
  for sequences, 121
Random sampling, 94–96
Rathje, William, 10
Recorded history, 51
Records of excavations, 100–101
Relative chronology, 40–51
  and artifacts, 41–45
  dating, see Chronometric dating
  and Ice Age, 47–51
  seriation techniques, see Seriation techniques

Religion
  beliefs, 164–167
  sites, *see* Religious sites
Religious sites, 33
  excavation of, 106–107
Remote sensing, 84–86
Research design for
      excavation, 91–93
Renfrew, Colin, 160
Resource base of sites, 81
Restivity survey meter,
      85–86
Rock art, 145–146
Rockshelters, excavation of,
      103
Rudenko, Sergei, 76

San. *See* !Kung San
Sampling, 94–96
Savagery stage, 12
Schliemann, Henrich, 80
Sea levels during
      Pleistocene, 50
Seriation techniques, 44–45
  illustration, 43
  in Tehuacán Valley, 46
Settlement archaeology,
      148–167
Settlements
  patterns, 68–70
  phases of, 121
Shadow sites, 82
Shakespeare, William, 39
Shang kings, burial of, 109
Shell middens, 106, 107, 144
Shell mounds, California, 30
Shellfish remains, 144
Shipwrecks, 9–10
Single-occupation sites, 41
Sites, 32–33
  accidental discoveries,
      86–88
  art sites, *see* Art sites
  burial sites, *see* Burial sites
  classifications of, 20
  excavations, *see*
      Excavations
  finding, 76–78
  habitation sites, *see*
      Habitation sites

hierarchies of, 157–159
interactions, 156–159
kill sites, *see* Kill sites
map of, 4–6
preservation of, 72–78
religious sites, *see*
      Religious sites
superposition and, 40–41
as unit of order, 120
Social anthropologists, 16
Social organization, 161–164
  and artifact patterning,
      162–164
Societies, 25
Space, 59–70
  and association, 61–63
Spaulding, Albert, 120
Speyer cathedral, 53
State-organized societies,
      162
Statistical sampling, 94–96
Stephens, John Lloyd, 80
Stereotypes of culture, 24
Stonehenge, England, 3, 33
Structures, 149–150
Struever, Stuart, 92–93, 141
Subassemblages, 63, 65–66
  illustration of, 68
Subsistence, 131–146
Subsystems in culture, 27
Sumerians, 12–13
  ecology of culture, 130
Superposition, 40–41
  illustration, 42
Surveys, 32, 78–88
  accidental discoveries,
      86–88
  aerial photography, 82–84
  remote sensing, 84–86
Stylistic types, 118–119
Swanscombe stone axes, 73
Systems, cultural, 26–27

Tahitians, 16
Tasmanians, 14
Taxonomy. *See*
      Classifications
Tehuacán Valley
  Coxcatlán Cave, 96
  plant remains, 141

seriation techniques, 46
Tells, excavation of, 104
Temple of Amun, Karnak,
    Egypt, 33
Tenochtitlán, 81, 86–87
Teosinte, 141
Teotihuacán Valley, 32,
    151–152
  excavation of, 106–107
  migration in, 129
  occupation of, 39, 40
  preservation of, 77
  restoration of, 3
  surveys of, 81
Tepe Yahya, Iran, 104
Thomsen, Christian
    Jurgensen, 123
Tierra del Fuegan Indians,
    12, 14
Tigris river, 13
Tikal, 33, 34
Time, 38–58
Tollund man, 74, 75, 134
Tombs. *See* Burial sites
Tools for excavation, 100
Tourism, 3, 7
Trade, 159–161
Tree-ring dating, 52–54
  and radiocarbon dating, 56
Trenches, 96–97, 99
Tribes, 162
Trier cathedral, 53
Trigger, Bruce, 149
Trobriand Islands, 16
Troy, 80
Tsoelike River, 145
Tsoelike rockshelter, 145
Tucson, Arizona garbage
    project, 10

Tutankhamun, 30–31, 32
  and association, 63
  preservation of tomb, 74
Tylor, Edward, 12–13, 14
Types, 116–120

Undergraduate degrees, 182
Underwater archaeologists,
    9–10
Units of ordering, 120–125
Ur-of-the-Chaldees, 32, 104,
    109
  social organization of, 162
Ussher, Archbishop James,
    11
Uxmal, 80

Vegetable remains, 139–142
Venus figurines, 164, 165
Vertical excavation, 96–97
Virú Valley, 21
  aerial photograph of, 84

Warren, Claude, 144
Waterlogged sites, 74
Wheeler, Mortimer, 105
White, Leslie, 26
Wild animals, 135–136
Willey, Gordon R., 21, 84
Williamsburg, Virginia, 8–9
Wodehouse, P. G., 90
Woolley, Leonard, 162

Yellen, John, 172

Zulu migrations, 129
Zuni Indians, 17, 19